THE POWER OF YOUR WORDS

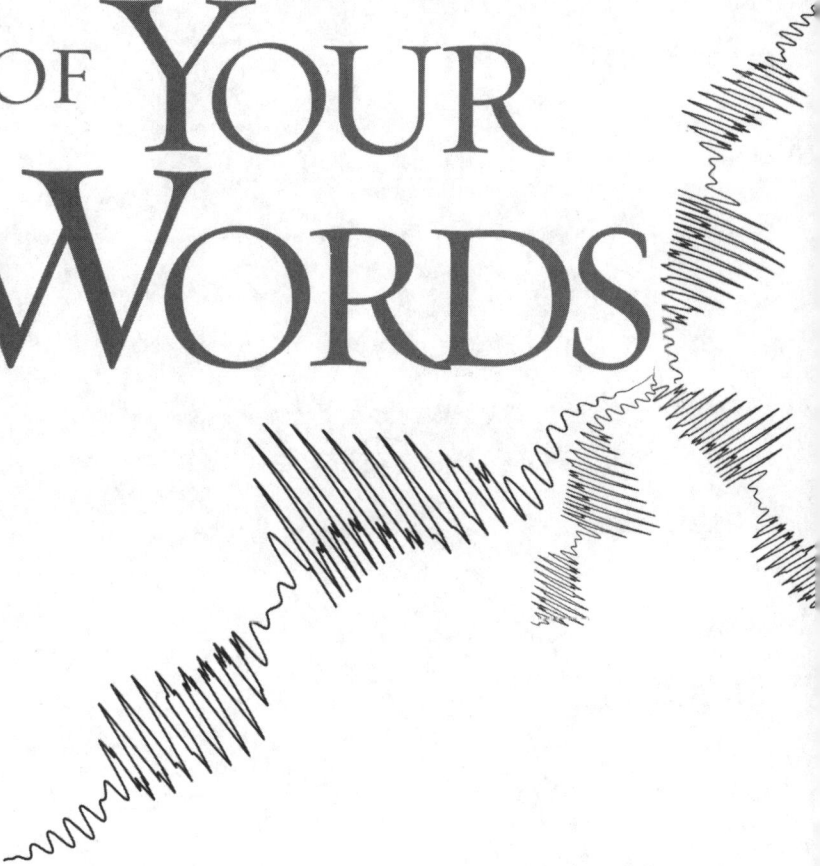

THE
POWER
OF YOUR
WORDS

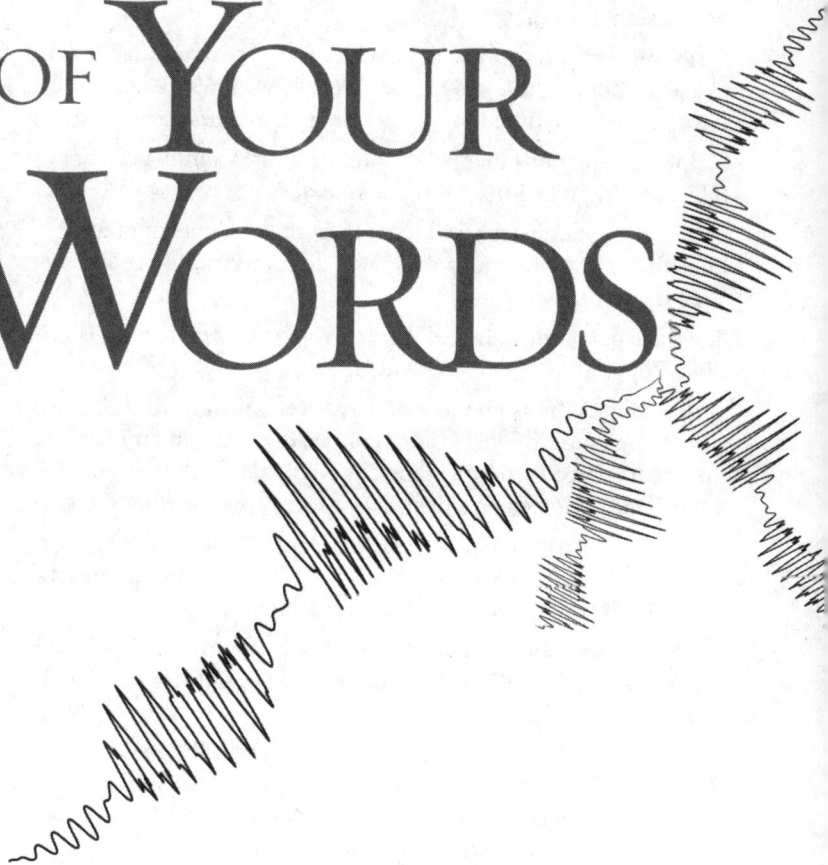

JOHN ECKHARDT

CHARISMA HOUSE

For more resources like this, visit MyCharismaShop.com and the author's website at apostleje.com.

Cataloging-in-Publication Data is on file with the Library of Congress.

International Standard Book Number: 978-1-63641-562-8
E-book ISBN: 978-1-63641-563-5

1 2025
Printed in the United States of America

Most Charisma Media products are available at special quantity discounts for bulk purchase for sales promotions, premiums, fundraising, and educational needs. For details, call us at (407) 333-0600 or visit our website at charismamedia.com.

Portions of this book were previously published by Charisma House as *Activate Heaven*, ISBN 978-1-62999-862-6, copyright © 2021; *The Prophet's Manual*, ISBN 978-1-62999-093-4, copyright © 2017; and *Prayers That Rout Demons*, ISBN 978-1-59979-246-0, copyright © 2008.

CONTENTS

INTRODUCTION

A s a speaker and author, I value words. Words are an important part of my life. This book is about the power of words, highlighting their influence, significance, and the impact they have through Scripture. God has a lot to say about words, and a revelation of the power of words will transform your life.

For years I've been diving deep into the incredible power our words hold. And honestly I have experienced that incredible power in my own life, seeing how speaking with faith and truth can shape someone's whole life. The truth about the power of words comes straight from Scripture, and God knows best about this subject. When you gain a revelation of this subject, it will not only change your life but also help you live abundantly.

A person speaks around sixteen thousand words per day, although that number fluctuates depending on gender, personality, environment, and profession.[1] A person hears tens of thousands of words daily, especially in conversation-rich or media-heavy settings. Words play a major role in our lives.

We often take words for granted. We can be slack and careless in our use of them. But God has called us to be careful with our words because words are powerful. Words are important, and understanding their influence will help you use them to benefit yourself and others. Speaking the right words and eliminating the wrong words will greatly enhance your life.

Expanding your vocabulary has benefits. This is true not only naturally but also spiritually. The benefits include enhanced communication skills, increased clarity, better comprehension, improved cognitive ability, and expanded learning. When you increase your vocabulary with the Word of God, it will enhance your ability to grasp and understand the workings of the Spirit.

Words matter. Studying this topic has given me a new appreciation for the power of words. I discovered insights while writing this book that I had never fully seen or understood before. For instance, words have the power to bless and benefit or to hurt and harm—they can work for you or against you.

Words matter. They matter to God, and they matter to others.

Your Voice Can Save a Generation

The call of God can save a generation. It can save families and individuals. And it can save you. God has an assignment—a calling—tailored specifically for you. God has a word He wants to put inside you that is not just for you but for your generation. When you obey that word and answer that call, you bring salvation, blessing, and deliverance to the people God sends you to—even to those you may not like.

Your voice can save a generation.

What if they don't listen? Whether they accept you and

your ministry, or the word you bring, is between them and God. The Book of Ezekiel says,

> When I say to the wicked, "You shall surely die," and you give him no warning, nor speak to warn the wicked from his wicked way, to save his life, that same wicked man shall die in his iniquity; but his blood I will require at your hand. Yet, if you warn the wicked, and he does not turn from his wickedness, nor from his wicked way, he shall die in his iniquity; but you have delivered your soul.
>
> —EZEKIEL 3:18–19, NKJV

Yes, there may be those who reject what God has sent you to say or do on His behalf, and they may end up being judged. But those who do receive it will be saved and delivered by Him. Don't run from your assignment to be and do all that God has called you to be and do. Embrace it and obey Him, and He will take care of the rest.

Your voice can save a generation.

In this hour of history, words are more important than ever. Words matter. Your words matter. But it is not just any words that carry importance; it is the words from the Word of God—words of truth, grace, mercy, warning, compassion, love, and hope—that matter most and have the capacity to save a generation.

—◊◊◊—

At the close of each chapter, you will find a QR code like the following one that will connect you to video teachings, prayers, and declarations designed to help you go even deeper into the revelation of the power of your words. I encourage you to take a moment to scan them as you read. They will enrich your reading experience, reinforce what you are learning, and deepen your faith.

JohnEckhardtBooks.com/resources

CHAPTER 1

WORDS MATTER

THE BIBLE USES terms such as *words, mouth, tongue, speech,* and *lips* to describe the power of words:

The words of a man's mouth are as deep waters, and the wellspring of wisdom as a flowing brook.

—PROVERBS 18:4

Let no corrupt communication proceed out of your mouth, but that which is good to the use of edifying, that it may minister grace unto the hearers.

—EPHESIANS 4:29

A wholesome tongue is a tree of life: but perverseness therein is a breach in the spirit.

—PROVERBS 15:4

For they that are such serve not our Lord Jesus Christ, but their own belly; and by good words and fair speeches deceive the hearts of the simple.

—ROMANS 16:18

The lips of the righteous feed many: but fools die for want of wisdom.

—PROVERBS 10:21

Words matter. Words are powerful. Words have an impact.

- Jonah's words resulted in an entire city repenting (Jon. 3).

- Paul's words caused Felix to tremble (Acts 24:25).

- Stephen's words angered the religious mob (Acts 7).

- Nebuchadnezzar's words brought judgment from heaven (Dan. 4).

- Job's friends' words kindled God's anger (Job 42).

- Three thousand souls responded to Peter's message on the day of Pentecost (Acts 2:41).

- David spoke words of faith before killing Goliath (1 Sam. 17:45–47).

- Samuel's words did not fall to the ground (1 Sam. 3:19).

- The Canaanite woman's words to Jesus released a miracle for her daughter (Matt. 15:22–28).

- The centurion's words to Jesus released a miracle for his servant (Matt. 8:5–13).

- Joseph's words to Pharaoh saved Egypt (Gen. 41).

- Esther's words delivered Israel from Haman (Est. 7–8).

- Solomon's words revealed his great wisdom (1 Kings 4:34; 10:24).

- Jezebel's words caused Elijah to hide (1 Kings 19:1–4).

- Rabshakeh's words brought fear to Jerusalem (2 Kings 18:19–19:3).

An interesting truth about the power of words is that even words from a non-Christian can be used to make a point about the truth of God. In Titus 1:12, Paul quoted the Cretan poet and philosopher Epimenides: "One of themselves, even a prophet of their own, said, the Cretans are always liars, evil beasts, slow bellies." Epimenides was a figure from ancient Crete known for his wisdom and sometimes paradoxical statements.

The specific line Paul quoted is a well-known fragment attributed to him. When Paul wrote, "One of themselves, even a prophet of their own..." he was referring to Epimenides as a respected figure within Cretan culture, even considering him a kind of prophet or wise man by their standards. This is interesting because Paul used a statement from a non-Christian, even one with a seemingly negative portrayal of the author's own people, the Cretans, to support his point about the need for firm leadership and correction within the church in Crete. He acknowledged the truth in Epimenides's assessment of Cretan character, likely to emphasize the seriousness of the issues Titus needed to address.

Even words from a non-Christian can be used to make a point about the truth of God.

The following are terms in Scripture that are notable and important to believers:

Christ	grace
the Father	glory
Abba	peace
sin	humility
flesh	fear of the Lord
judgment	wisdom
the cross	calling
faith	election
righteousness	Zion
love	justified
mercy	new creation
heaven	kingdom
hell	the church
Holy Spirit	praise
heart	worship
holiness	covenant
forgiveness	blood
gospel	mysteries
prayer	salvation
Word of God	eternal life
truth	

Understanding these words is essential to understanding our faith. They will remain significant from generation to generation.

WORDS AS WINDOWS

The words we choose serve as windows into our thoughts, beliefs, and values. Our vocabulary, our tone, and the subjects we discuss reveal aspects of our character and inner state. Careful speech reflects a thoughtful and considerate mind, while impulsive or negative language can indicate underlying anger, insecurity, or prejudice. By paying attention to our word choices, we can gain valuable insights into our inner landscape and identify areas for personal growth.

Psalm 34:12–14 says, "What man is he that desireth life, and loveth many days, that he may see good? Keep thy tongue from evil, and thy lips from speaking guile. Depart from evil, and do good; seek peace, and pursue it." In other words, if you desire to see many good days, you need to pay attention to your words and speak what is good and true. An evil and deceitful tongue will bring trouble, as your words shape the course of your life.

When you speak evil things, you attract evil to your life.

When you speak evil things, you attract evil to your life. In Hebrew the term *lashon hara*—evil tongue—refers to speech that causes harm, including gossip and defaming someone by revealing negative details about them.[1] This kind of speech often leads to trouble in relationships. The Bible has much to say about gossip and slander: Avoid it, keep your tongue from speaking it, and don't let it come out of your mouth. Wisdom teaches us to avoid evil speaking because words matter.

THE POWER OF WORDS IN THE BOOK OF JOB

The Book of Job emphasizes the power of words, highlighting their potential for both comfort and destruction, and underscores the importance of speaking with wisdom and discernment. The narrative explores the impact of words on Job's suffering and the efforts of his friends to console him; their seemingly well-intentioned words often proved more hurtful than helpful.

No other book in the Bible features a dialogue between friends quite like the Book of Job. The term *words* appears thirty-nine times in Job—more than every other book of the Bible except Jeremiah. Job is, in essence, a book about the power of words.

The Book of Job has five human speakers, each demonstrating the power of words. Three of them are Job's friends, who came to comfort him. While comfort was their original intent, the purpose behind their words changed as they spoke. Instead of comforting Job, Job's friends began to accuse him of hidden sin, and their words afflicted him even more.

Miserable comforters

Job's friends' limited understanding of what had taken place in the spirit realm hindered them from speaking prophetically into the situation. Their speeches fell short because their understanding fell short. Instead of helping Job, they added to his frustration and pain, making matters worse. Our words can hurt even when our intention is to help.

Words intended for good can be deeply damaging if they lack empathy, fail to consider the individual's context, or are rooted in flawed assumptions. With their words Job's friends attempted to define his reality and assign blame without concrete evidence. This demonstrates the power of language to frame situations and influence beliefs, even when those beliefs are harmful or wrong. Job's friends' unwavering certainty in their theological frameworks prevented them from truly empathizing with Job's pain and led them to use words that wounded rather than healed.

Job called his friends "miserable comforters" (Job 16:2), stating that their words were vain, or empty (v. 3). The Hebrew phrase translated as "miserable comforters" implies not only that they failed to comfort him, but also that they actually added to his misery—as if they were working at it.[2] Their presence should have brought peace and empathy; instead, they became sources of further torment.

A person's suffering is intensified when others speak with an authority that exceeds their actual knowledge. Job's friends, rigidly clinging to their simplistic formula that equated sin with suffering and righteousness with prosperity, demonstrated this. Despite having no genuine understanding of why Job was enduring such hardship, they confidently fabricated reasons for his plight, presenting their assumptions as absolute truths. Their pronouncements, born not of empathy but of unwavering adherence to their narrow worldview, only deepened Job's misery by dismissing the complexity of his situation due to the limits of their own understanding.

> *A person's suffering is intensified when others speak with an authority that exceeds their actual knowledge.*

That is why Job asked, "How long will ye vex my soul, and break me in pieces with words?" (Job 19:2). Job's words revealed his pain and confusion, his grief and struggle. Job felt like he was being treated unfairly. He accused his friends of heaping up words against him (Job 16:4). He stated that if they were in his place, he would strengthen and comfort them with his mouth (v. 5).

Job's pain was so great that he cursed the day he was born (Job 3:3). His words are striking: "Let those curse it who curse the day, who are skilled in rousing up Leviathan" (Job 3:8, AMPC). This phrase refers to professional mourners or magicians in the ancient world—those believed to have the power to pronounce curses or perform rituals that could alter the natural order. To rouse Leviathan was to summon uncontrollable forces of darkness and chaos. Job was essentially saying, "Let those with the power to unleash cosmic chaos curse the day I was born." Job's words revealed deep hurt and pain. And Job wasn't the only one in the Bible to curse the day he was born; the prophet Jeremiah cursed the day he was born too (Jer. 20:14–18).

Crushing words

Words can crush a spirit—perhaps more than any other action or activity. All three of Job's friends cut him with their words. Job had wanted an honest hearing, but his friends came with a preconceived theology that prejudiced their thinking about Job's situation. Their words of judgment cut him to pieces. Job felt humiliated and mistreated because of their words (Job 19:3).

What makes Job's situation even more painful was that Job was an encourager. This is what Eliphaz, one of Job's three friends, said about him: "Behold, thou hast instructed many, and thou hast strengthened the weak hands. Thy words have upholden him that was falling, and thou hast strengthened the feeble knees" (Job 4:3–4). Another translation says, "Your words have supported those who were falling; you encouraged those with shaky knees" (v. 4, NLT). Job encouraged many people, and yet he did not receive encouragement from his friends in return. And that is not all. Job "delivered the poor that cried, and the fatherless, and him that had none to help him" (Job 29:12). He "caused the widow's heart to sing for joy" (Job 29:13). Job was "eyes to the blind, and feet…to the lame" (Job 29:15). Job "was a father to the poor" (Job 29:16). Job was a great encourager to all kinds of people.

Imagine if Job's friend circle had looked a little different.

What if he had a close companion, someone who also had a knack for lifting others' spirits? During that devastating time when Job lost everything—his children, his animals, his very health—a friend with a similar encouraging spirit could have made a world of difference. We've all had periods when one bad thing seems to follow another, and that's the kind of relentless hardship Job faced. So how might an encouraging friend have stepped in? If he had a friend who recognized the power of encouraging words, what kind of support could they have offered?

Inspired words

Elihu, a younger man who had been listening to Job and his three friends, was the last person to speak before God had His turn. Elihu was not rebuked by Job or God for his statements. Elihu claimed to be filled with the Spirit of God and to speak on God's behalf (Job 32:8; 36:2-3), which was proven true when God began to speak. If you compare what Elihu said with the Word of God, it is clear that Elihu spoke by inspiration. Inspired words are true and worthy to be spoken. We should speak by inspiration.

Job's wish was for his words to be written down (Job 19:23). He wanted generations to come to hear his words and understand his feelings. He felt his words were important to hear. This is a powerful expression of the human need to be heard, to be understood, and to have one's story preserved. Our words are important, and we want to be heard. Words matter.

Some words are worth preserving, especially inspired words. The Bible preserves words spoken thousands of years ago. The founding documents and constitutions of nations are preserved. The great speeches of great men are preserved.

Great works of literature are preserved. These words still inspire us and give us direction today.

Thankfully Job's words have been written down and preserved. The words of Jesus changed the course of history. Thankfully they are preserved. These words are powerful and life changing.

Incorrectly spoken words

Ultimately the Book of Job suggests that human language may be insufficient to comprehend the complexities of divine justice and suffering. Our words are limited by what we know. When God began to speak to Job, He first asked, "Who is this that darkeneth counsel by words without knowledge?" (Job 38:2). Only God can give us words and insight beyond our human understanding.

That's also why "after the LORD had spoken these words unto Job, the LORD said to Eliphaz the Temanite, My wrath is kindled against thee, and against thy two friends: for ye have not spoken of me the thing that is right, as my servant Job hath" (Job 42:7). This was God's response. He was angry with Job's friends and rebuked them sharply since their words were not good. This shows that we can speak words that are wrong, even though we are convinced they are right. The friends had to offer a burnt offering, and Job had to pray for his friends (Job 42:8). His prayer delivered them from God's judgment.

When our knowledge is limited, our words should be limited.

The Book of Job shows the power—and consequences—of words spoken incorrectly. It reveals that many words are not spoken rightly, especially in times of testing, trial, and grief. We need God's wisdom to speak the right thing at the right time. When our knowledge is limited, our words should be limited. Too many speeches are made without wisdom and understanding, and too often people speak on matters for which they are not qualified. That's why Scripture cautions us: "Talk no more so exceeding proudly; let not arrogancy come out of your mouth: for the LORD is a God of knowledge, and by him actions are weighed" (1 Sam. 2:3).

Leviathan is the subject of Job chapter 41. Leviathan is identified as "a king over all the children of pride" (Job 41:34). Leviathan is also associated with chaos and confusion. Pride and confusion are problems with many who speak. Many words are rooted in pride—and those are words spoken incorrectly. We must walk in humility. We must speak with humility. God weighs words. God resists the proud (Jas. 4:6).

Diagnostic words

The Book of Job describes in detail Job's sickness and pain. It contains the most descriptive account of physical infirmity found in Scripture. The book teaches us that words are more than sounds; they are containers of experience. When someone is in deep distress—whether physical, emotional, or spiritual—words become the means by which pain is processed and exposed. Job's story teaches us that while it's not wrong to verbalize pain, we must guard against building a theology of defeat from temporary suffering. Faith must eventually rise and speak.

Here is a list of Job's infirmities:

- Sore boils from head to toe (Job 2:7): Painful boils covered Job's entire body, from the crown of his head to his feet.

- Constant itching and scraping (Job 2:8): Job used broken pottery to scrape his skin, indicating unbearable irritation.

- Disfigurement and altered appearance (Job 2:12): His appearance was so changed that his friends didn't recognize him.

- Severe pain and cramping (Job 6:4): Job described his suffering as poisoned arrows piercing his spirit.

- Sleeplessness, insomnia, and restlessness (Job 7:4): Restless nights offered no relief due to pain and anxiety.

- Worms (Job 7:5): His sores became infested with worms.

- Cracking and bleeding skin (Job 7:5): He had broken, likely infected, and oozing skin.

- Weakness and physical exhaustion (Job 16:7): He felt utterly drained and weary.

- Wrinkles and leanness of face (Job 16:8): Job had visibly aged and was emaciated due to suffering.

- Weeping and impaired vision (Job 16:16): Swollen eyelids and blurred vision were caused from excessive crying.

- Foul breath (Job 19:17): This was likely due to internal distress or infection.

- Weight loss and emaciation (Job 19:20): He lost so much weight that only skin and bone remained.

- Foul odor and physical decay (Job 30:10): Others recoiled from Job because of his smell and appearance.

- Bones, tendons, and nerves in constant agony (Job 30:17): He suffered unrelenting pain throughout his body, especially at night.

- Fever or burning skin (Job 30:30): He had a high fever or inflammation described as his bones burning with heat.

- Skin blackened (Job 30:30): Blackened and bruised skin indicated the severity of Job's condition.

- Organ/internal pain (Job 30:31): Job's "organ" turning to weeping implies distress in his internal organs.

Job's recognition of his total physical decline and human frailty caused him to say, "Man that is born of a woman is of few days and full of trouble" (Job 14:1).

Just as doctors listen to a patient's words to diagnose illness, we can hear the spiritual condition of a person by what they say. In Luke 6:45, Jesus said that out "of the abundance of the heart his mouth speaketh." Job's words give us a prophetic window into his battle. His verbal descriptions weren't only diagnostic; they were part of the spiritual warfare. His words

Words show us the condition of people's hearts.

exposed not only his body's condition but his soul's torment and his cry for understanding. Words show us the condition of people's hearts.

SMALL BUT POWERFUL

Beware the tongue. James 3:5 says, "Even so the tongue is a little member, and boasteth great things. Behold, how great a matter a little fire kindleth!" Although it is one of the smallest parts of the body, it carries immense power. Do not be deceived by its size—for, despite its smallness, it can steer the course of a person's life. As the Scriptures warn, the tongue holds the power of life and death (Prov. 18:21). The small tongue can start a raging fire; large fires start small. They can begin with just a spark—with just one word spoken incorrectly. What seems insignificant can destroy relationships, stir up strife, or set your destiny ablaze. Handle your words with fear and wisdom.

You can keep your soul from trouble by keeping your tongue. Proverbs 21:23 says, "Whoso keepeth his mouth and his tongue keepeth his soul from troubles." This verse connects the tongue with trouble. The Hebrew word for *keep* means to guard, to keep watch, to have charge of, to refrain, and to beware. It carries the sense of putting a hedge around something to protect it.[3] You need to guard and take charge of what you say. This will keep you out of trouble, calamity, or disaster. Sometimes you will have to put the brakes on your tongue and guard what you say. You cannot afford to just say anything. You need to take responsibility for your mouth. You are responsible for your words and your life.

Your words affect your life—a careless talker destroys himself. Proverbs 13:3 says, "He that keepeth his mouth keepeth his life: but he that openeth wide his lips shall have destruction." This is another sobering verse about the tongue and its impact on your life. You can either keep or destroy your life with your words. God warns us about the danger of excessive talking or having a big mouth. It is better to limit your words than to speak too much.

One reason so many people face trouble in their lives is that their words—especially their excessive words—cause problems. Their trouble is as close as their mouths; they don't need to look far to find the source. Trouble begins with their words—it is as near as their tongue. But since the source is so close, they don't need to go far to fix it. They can change it by taking responsibility for their words, fixing their mouths, and changing their words.

When you control your tongue, you control your life.

That's why Psalm 141:3 says, "Set a watch, O LORD, before my mouth; keep the door of my lips." You can ask God to help you in this area— we all need His help. The psalmist's request is one we should all make, because God can and will help us. It is a prayer that many more people need to pray. Guarding our words is one of the most important areas to seek God's help in. You don't have to struggle alone; your life is at stake. Ask for and receive God's help in guarding your words—and avoid destruction.

When you control your tongue, you control your life. It is important not only to avoid speaking evil but also to speak good things. At times it is equally important to refrain from speaking. Don't be irresponsible in your speech; take responsibility for what comes out of your mouth. Discipline yourself to speak noble and excellent things. Learn to speak what is true, just, pure, and lovely. Learn to speak what is right.

SPEAK LIFE

A wholesome tongue is a gentle and kind tongue. Proverbs 15:4 says, "A wholesome tongue is a tree of life: but perverseness therein is a breach in the spirit." Words can heal or destroy. Kind words are like medicine, while evil words can break and crush the spirit. Many people suffer with broken spirits because of unkind and cruel words. You cannot enjoy life with a broken spirit—a broken spirit dries the bones (Prov. 17:22), resulting in depression, health issues, sickness, and even premature death. Many health issues stem from harmful words. Words can bring life or death.

Don't be foolish with your speech. Foolish speech brings destruction. The Book of Proverbs speaks about wisdom and foolishness: "A fool's mouth is his destruction, and his lips are the snare of his soul" (18:7). Foolish speech will cause you to fall into a snare—a snare is a trap, typically with a noose. Proverbs 6:2 says, "Thou art snared with the words of thy mouth, thou art taken with the words of thy mouth." Don't be trapped by your words. Don't allow your words to put a noose around your neck. Don't make promises you can't keep. Be careful what you promise. Be careful of the commitments you make with your words. Don't be hung by your tongue.

To speak excellent things, you must have command over your mouth. Proverbs 8:6 says, "Hear; for I will speak of excellent things; and the opening of my lips shall be right things." *Right* means morally good, justified, or acceptable. The English word *excellent* means extremely good or outstanding. However, the Hebrew word translated "excellent things" means commander.[4]

In my study on words, I was amazed at how much the Book of Proverbs speaks about words, the tongue, and speech. Proverbs is a book of wisdom. "Wisdom is the principal thing" (Prov. 4:7). In other words, wisdom is the most important thing, the primary thing, the foundational thing. We can also say that right speaking is the most important thing, since wisdom is connected to the tongue.

Principal also means beginning. In fact, the word for *principal* in Proverbs 4:7 is the same word used for *beginning* in Genesis 1:1.[5] If you want a good life, begin with your tongue. If you want to change your life, begin with your tongue. Your tongue is principal, primary, important, and foundational.

Proverbs 18:20 says, "A man's belly shall be satisfied with the fruit of his mouth; and with the increase of his lips shall he be filled." The word *belly* in Hebrew thought often symbolizes the inner being or the seat of appetite and satisfaction—not just physical hunger but the desires of life.[6] "With the increase of his lips shall he be filled" expands the idea—the more you speak wisely, righteously, and productively, the more you will see your life enriched and fulfilled.

Proverbs 18:20 teaches us that a person will "eat," or experience, the consequences of their speech, whether good or bad. What we say can build, bless, and benefit not only others but ourselves. What we say can also crush, curse, and condemn not only others but ourselves. That is why the next verse states that death and life are in the power of the tongue. There is a connection. Your words are not empty and void; they have the power to affect your life positively or negatively.

"Death and life are in the power of the tongue: and they that love it shall eat the fruit thereof" (Prov. 18:21). This is a principal verse on the power of words. The tongue is important because it determines death or life. It is so important to understand this verse and walk in an understanding of it. Your words affect your life. Your words affect the lives of others. Your words can cause death or life. What an amazing power your words have! But that also means you carry an important responsibility with your words. Your words matter.

Many people are not responsible with their words. Many are too careless with their speech. This carelessness can cost you your life. Careless speech can cause you to lose your peace. Words of death can cause you to self-sabotage your life and destiny. Don't be careless with your words. Govern your tongue. Bridle your mouth. Take command of your speech. This is the way to ensure many good days.

You must restrain your tongue. Psalm 39:1 says, "I said, I will take heed to my ways, that I sin not with my tongue: I will keep my mouth with a bridle, while the wicked is before me." The phrase *bridle the tongue* means to control or restrain one's speech, to speak carefully and intentionally, and to avoid saying things that are hurtful, inappropriate, or harmful. It suggests practicing self-control and thinking before speaking, emphasizing the power of words to both build up and tear down. The modern word *bridle* comes from the Old English word *bridel,* meaning restraint.[7] You cannot allow yourself to say words that hurt your well-being. You should not speak words that hurt others. A lack of restraint can bring self-destruction, and it can also destroy others.

Careless speech can cause you to lose your peace.

We all need knowledge regarding the mouth and tongue. Proverbs 17:27–28 says, "He that hath knowledge spareth his words: and a man of understanding is of an excellent spirit. Even a fool, when he holdeth his peace, is counted wise: and he that shutteth his lips is esteemed a man of understanding." Ignorance of these truths will bring destruction. With this knowledge, spare your words. Doing so is a sign of an excellent spirit. Even fools are considered wise when quiet. In other words, even if you are foolish, no one will know it if you keep your mouth shut.

Wisdom is speaking to us in Proverbs. Wisdom leads to success. Wisdom warns us about the dangers of foolish speaking. Wisdom gives us a master key to success and blessing. Your tongue and your words are keys to a good life.

Keys open and unlock doors. I am convinced that right words can give you access. I am also convinced that wrong words can shut doors. We all need open doors in life. We all need opportunities. Let your tongue turn the lock. Let your tongue open the door.

Refrain your lips. Proverbs 10:19 says, "In the multitude of words there wanteth not sin: but he that refraineth his lips is wise." Be careful not to speak too much. Do not sin with your words. Sin can be found in the multitude of words.

Avoid speaking lies. Proverbs 8:7 says, "For my mouth shall speak truth; and wickedness is an abomination to my lips." This is wisdom speaking. Wisdom speaks truth. Wisdom hates wicked speech. It is important to speak truth. Do not allow dishonesty to be in your mouth. Truth must be a priority in your life.

Learn to speak truth, and learn the power of truthful words. Proverbs 12:19 says, "The lip of truth shall be established for ever: but a lying tongue is but for a moment." Truth will always be true. Lies cannot last forever. Your tongue can be a conduit of truth or a conduit of lies. God's Word is truth. Truth is liberating. True words keep you free.

Many people do not know what is acceptable. Ecclesiastes 12:10 says, "The preacher sought to find out acceptable words: and that which was written was upright, even words of truth." Acceptable words are right and pleasant words. Truth should always be acceptable. Are your words acceptable? Are your words appropriate? Acceptable words are profitable words. Do your words profit you and others? Do your words benefit you and others? Your words can give you an advantage, or your words can put you at a disadvantage.

David understood that speech has power, and he wrote in this psalm that he desired that what came out of his mouth would honor God. Psalm 19:14 says, "Let the words of my mouth, and the meditation of my heart, be acceptable in thy sight, O LORD, my strength, and my redeemer." Are your words acceptable to God? Are your words pleasing to God? Do your words honor God? God listens to your words. There is much speech that is not acceptable to God. God hears what is spoken in secret. God weighs our words. Words matter.

JohnEckhardtBooks.com/chp1

CHAPTER 2

THE POWER
OF WORDS

WORDS ARE POWERFUL. Words have impact. Luke 4:32 says, "And they were astonished at [Jesus'] doctrine: for his word was with power." Jesus spoke with power. His words were authoritative. The people were astonished. They were amazed at His words. Words can astonish when spoken with power. Words are containers for the power of God. Words are conduits of power.

Creation began with words. God spoke the words, and there was light. God used words to create the earth and everything in it (Gen. 1).

Words are the tools of preachers, teachers, statesmen, presidents, prime ministers, governors, singers, activists, generals, coaches, and leaders. Words have been the foundation of important speeches throughout history.

Words give vision. Words are used by visionaries. Leaders use words to cast vision. We release vision through words, and we receive vision through words.

Words paint a picture. Words give us the ability to see things. Words open our eyes.

Words have significance (1 Cor. 14:10). Words have meaning. Words help us express what we think and feel.

Words are used in prayer (1 Tim. 2:1).

Angels respond to words. When Daniel prayed, an angel came in response: "Then said he unto me, Fear not, Daniel: for from the first day that thou didst set thine heart to understand, and to chasten thyself before thy God, thy words were heard, and I am come for thy words" (Dan. 10:12).

"A soft tongue breaks the bone" (Prov. 25:15, MEV). This is a poetic expression of the power of gentle speech. "Bone" represents something hard, resistant, or unyielding. "Soft tongue" refers to kind, gentle, measured, and wise words. Even kind and gentle words are powerful.

Words release destiny. Words can direct the course of our lives. Just as a small rudder steers a large ship, the tongue can set the direction of one's life (Jas. 3:4–5).

Words are spirit. Our words can come from the Holy Spirit (John 6:63). Words can touch and affect our spirits.

Words reveal purity. Words reveal the heart. What is in the heart will be heard by the ear through words, for out of the abundance of the heart the mouth speaks (Luke 6:45). Pureness of speech reveals pureness of heart.

Words should be tested—not blindly accepted.

We make promises and commitments with words. Vows and pledges are made with words.

Words can travel around the world quickly. Words can be heard throughout the earth (Ps. 19:4).

Words release prosperity. Words help us succeed. Words teach us to profit.

Our words should be seasoned with salt (Col. 4:6). To speak with salt is to make our words meaningful, preserving what is good and challenging what is corrupt.

Words should be tested—not blindly accepted. People have a moral and spiritual responsibility to discern what they hear, just as they instinctively know what tastes good or bad (Job 12:11).

Words can drop like rain, bringing blessing and refreshing (Job 29:22). Moses's speech dropped like rain (Deut. 32:2).

Words and deeds go together (Rom. 15:18). Paul not only preached but demonstrated the power of God in deeds.

Words reveal snakes. Jesus called the Pharisees a generation of vipers. They could not say good things. Their words revealed they were snakes (Matt. 12:34).

Words can trouble the hearer (2 Thess. 2:2). The wrong words can disturb the mind and disturb peace.

Words can cause strife and division (1 Tim. 6:4). This is usually a result of pride.

We command with words. Jesus commanded the wind and the water through words (Luke 8:25). Demons are commanded to come out through words.

We decree with words (Job 22:28). A decree is an authoritative command. Kings issued decrees through words.

We rebuke with words. Jesus rebuked devils with his words (Matt. 17:18). The word *rebuke* means to speak sternly.

We communicate with words. Business is conducted through words. Transactions are completed through words. Words make the world go around. Words are used in transactions. Words are used in diplomacy and negotiations. Words are used in arts and entertainment. Words are used in announcements. Words are used in commentaries, discussions, and debates.

The words we use to describe situations, others, and ourselves influence how we think and feel about them.

Words can elicit a wide range of emotions: joy, sorrow, anger, fear, love, and empathy.

Words can build and destroy relationships. Words connect us and build intimacy.

Words can be persuasive. Words can convince.

Words are catalysts. Words cause a reaction.

Words are the foundation of libraries and accumulated knowledge. Words provide a storehouse and treasury of thoughts and minds.

Words have power to penetrate the inner recesses of our hearts, leaving scars that wound us for life and even shape our identities (Prov. 12:18).

Words are the tools of authors. At the root, an author is not just a writer but a creator, originator, or initiator of something—whether ideas, stories, movements, or meaning. This reflects the powerful idea that authors don't just record; they cause things to come into being.

Signs and wonders follow words (Mark 16:20).

Words raised the dead (John 11:43). Lazarus came forth when Jesus spoke.

Idols don't have words. They do not speak. They are dumb (1 Cor. 12:2).

Words can be anointed. Jesus was anointed to preach and proclaim deliverance to the captives. The power and anointing of the Spirit were in His words (Luke 4:18–19).

Words give the ability to know history. Words help us remember the past. Books in Scripture record the history of redemption. Two books, called Chronicles, focus on this history. A chronicle is a factual written account of important or historical events in the order of their occurrence. We need words to chronicle and record. The scribes in Israel were meticulous with words. They had to record every jot and tittle. "Jot and tittle" is an idiom meaning every detail, no matter how small. Hebrew words were picture words. The words expressed more than a simple thought. Even the letters in the Hebrew language were pictures.

We praise with words. Praise is powerful. Praise stills the enemy and the avenger. Praises looses confusion into the camp of the enemy.

We magnify God with words. We thank God with words. God creates the praise of the lips. In other words, God gives us the words to release to Him in praise. Isaiah 57:19 says, "I create the fruit of the lips; Peace, peace to him that is far off, and to him that is near, saith the LORD; and I will heal him." Another translation of this verse says, "I will teach them a new word" (ERV). We can sing songs by inspiration, placed in our mouths by God. We can sing new songs, for God gives us new words to sing. These songs and words release new things in our lives.

We live by the words that proceed from God's mouth (Deut. 8:3; Matt. 4:4).

WHAT WORDS BRING

Words bring wisdom, knowledge, and understanding. We explain ideas through words. We understand subjects through words. Many subjects have words that are used for that subject alone. We learn through words. We are taught through words. We read words. We counsel and give advice with words. Words are a conduit for wisdom. Wisdom is transferred from generation to generation with words. Words are the instruments of the wise.

Words bring salvation. Words are used to preach the gospel. Words bring glad tidings and good news. The gospel is the power of God unto salvation.

Words bring hope. Words create expectation. Words give us hope for the future. Words uplift the hopeless.

Words bring joy. Good news brings joy. Words can affect our happiness. "The joy of the LORD is your strength" (Neh. 8:10). Joyful words can strengthen us.

Words bring faith (Rom. 10:17). We believe what is spoken.

Words bring truth. Truth is spoken and received through words (Eph. 4:15).

Words bring peace. Words are what peacemakers use to bring peace. Peace treaties are words that are signed and agreed upon.

Words bring correction. Words bring adjustment to our lives.

Words bring change and transformation. Words change things. Words turn things around.

Words bring revelation. Words reveal mysteries and help us understand parables (Prov. 1:6).

Words bring healing and deliverance. Jesus cast out the spirits and healed all who were sick with His words (Matt. 8:16).

Words bring comfort. Words comfort and restore the brokenhearted (Luke 4:18).

Words bring confirmation. Judas and Silas confirmed the churches with many words (Acts 15:32).

WORDS ARE SEEDS

Words are seeds. Words are planted in the heart. Seeds, although small, have the power to multiply. Seeds contain the power to grow and expand. Seeds have the power to break through. The planted seed is a natural wonder. Words carry the same power. Words, like seeds, can seem insignificant until they are planted.

Words produce a harvest. They are the seeds that eventually produce a harvest. Words operate according to the law of seedtime and harvest (Gen. 8:22). We reap what we sow. We reap what we speak. If you want a different harvest, then change your words.

Words have power to convict and pierce the heart. The people were pricked in their hearts when they heard the message of Peter (Acts 2:37).

Words can start movements and revivals. Words can draw people to God.

Words impart. Timothy received a gift through words (1 Tim. 4:14).

Words build up. Words edify (Eph. 4:29). Words are the building blocks of life.

Words shape the way we think and act. We are shaped by what we hear in life.

Words refresh. Good news brings refreshing (Prov. 25:25).

Words provide direction. Words tell us where to go. Words help us find our way.

Words encourage. Words release courage to the discouraged. Words motivate us to move ahead.

Words inspire. Words motivate us. Words stir us.

Words activate. Words get things moving. Words awaken us. Words pique our curiosity.

Words challenge us to do great things. Words help us break limitations and move into new realms.

BLESSING AND CURSING

Words can produce blessing or cursing. Consider the power of blessing and cursing found throughout Scripture. In the Old Testament, blessings were often seen as having a tangible effect on the recipient's life, bestowing favor and prosperity. Conversely, curses carried the weight of misfortune. This highlights the spiritual force of words, which can influence the material world. Think of Isaac's blessing of Jacob (Gen. 27)—words that irrevocably altered the family's future.

The patriarchs understood the power of words used in blessing. The patriarchs desired blessing. Melchizedek blessed Abraham with words (Gen. 14:18–19). Balaam was hired by Balak to curse Israel with words, but he ended up blessing them instead (Num. 23:11). Isaac blessed Jacob with words. Jacob blessed his sons with words (Gen. 49), and Moses blessed the tribes of Israel with words (Deut. 33). The priests were told to bless Israel with words (Num. 6:24–26). Words are indeed powerful.

Scripture speaks of a generation that curses its father and mother (Prov. 30:11). These are words used in a dishonorable way. This is a sure sign of disobedience and rebellion. Blessing and cursing are two powerful forces that affect generations. Words affect destinies. Words can shape the future.

THE POWER OF FAITH-FILLED WORDS

Jesus showed us the tremendous power of faith-filled words when trees and storms responded to His words. Creation responds to words.

And he arose, and rebuked the wind, and said unto the sea, Peace, be still. And the wind ceased, and there was a great calm.

—MARK 4:39

And when he saw a fig tree in the way, he came to it, and found nothing thereon, but leaves only, and said unto it, Let no fruit grow on thee henceforward for ever. And presently the fig tree withered away.

—MATTHEW 21:19

When Joshua spoke words of faith, the sun and moon stayed still.

Then spake Joshua to the LORD in the day when the LORD delivered up the Amorites before the children of Israel, and he said in the sight of Israel, Sun, stand thou still upon Gibeon; and thou, Moon, in the valley of Ajalon.

And the sun stood still, and the moon stayed, until the people had avenged themselves upon their enemies. Is not this written in the book of Jasher? So the sun stood still in the midst of heaven, and hasted not to go down about a whole day.

—JOSHUA 10:12–13

Jesus taught,

For verily I say unto you, That whosoever shall say unto this mountain, Be thou removed, and be thou cast into the sea; and shall not doubt in his heart, but shall believe that those things which he saith shall come to pass; he shall have whatsoever he saith.

—MARK 11:23

This verse is one of the most powerful teachings Jesus gave on the authority of faith-filled words. It came immediately after Jesus cursed the fig tree and the disciples saw it withered from the roots—demonstrating the power of spoken faith.

Faith is released through words. Jesus mentioned the words *say* and *saith* three times and *believe* one time. The emphasis was on the word *saying*. You can have what you *say*. This is the culmination of the principle that what you consistently believe and declare with faith you will eventually see.

Those who understand this principle understand the power of words. Your words are containers of faith. Your mouth contains a miracle.

You speak what you believe in your heart. I call this the heart-mouth connection. Remember, out of the abundance of the heart the mouth speaks (Luke 6:45). Faith in the heart is released through the mouth. Faith comes by hearing. The words of faith you hear will get in your heart. What gets in your heart will proceed from your mouth. It's a cycle.

Second Corinthians 4:13 says, "We having the same spirit of faith, according as it is written, I believed, and therefore have I spoken; we also believe, and therefore speak." This verse reveals a profound principle: Faith operates not just by believing but also by confessing and speaking. Paul wrote to the Corinthians about enduring hardship while staying anchored in hope and victory. He connected their perseverance to a timeless truth: Faith speaks. This spirit of faith is released through words. We believe, and we speak—Paul calls this the spirit of faith.

He was quoting Psalm 116:10: "I believed, therefore have I spoken." This is a timeless principle, which works from generation to generation. One translation of 2 Corinthians 4:13 says,

"We boldly say what we believe" (TLB). Paul kept preaching and declaring despite persecution because he believed.

Romans 10:17–18 says, "So then faith cometh by hearing, and hearing by the word of God. But I say, Have they not heard? Yes verily, their sound went into all the earth, and their words unto the ends of the world." Words are necessary to receive and release faith. Faith comes by hearing the Word of God. People believe when they hear the gospel. Paul said the gospel had been preached in all the world. Notice the mention of "words" in verse 18. Paul quoted Psalm 19:4, which prophesied the words of the preacher going into all the world: "Their line is gone out through all the earth, and their words to the end of the world." The world heard "words." These words brought faith and salvation to many.

The words, the preaching, are called the word of faith: "The word is nigh thee, even in thy mouth, and in thy heart: that is, the word of faith, which we preach" (Rom. 10:8). The word of faith is nigh. It is near. It is not in heaven, far away, or in hell, far beneath. It is in your mouth and in your heart.

This is an important principle of faith: If you get the word in your mouth, you will get it in your heart. It's that heart-mouth connection. You believe from your heart. Words in your mouth will get in your heart. It will change your life.

Speaking the Word of God is the key to depositing the Word in your heart. Your heart becomes a treasury. You store the Word in the treasury of your heart. Remember, the issues of your life flow from your heart (Prov. 4:23).

SPEAK THE WORD

Matthew 8:8 says, "The centurion answered and said, Lord, I am not worthy that thou shouldest come under my roof: but speak the word only, and my servant shall be healed." The centurion received a miracle for his servant because he knew the power of words. He was a commander. He understood authority. When he gave an order, his soldiers responded. The centurion understood Jesus' authority, so he asked Jesus to speak the word only, knowing that was all it took for his servant to be healed. His servant was healed through a spoken word. When Jesus heard the centurion's declaration of faith, "he marvelled, and said to them that followed, Verily I say unto you, I have not found so great faith, no, not in Israel" (v. 10).

Faith-filled words are powerful. Faith-filled words release miracles. This is the word of faith. Faith is released out of your mouth. Faith is released through your words. This is true of salvation. Confession is made unto salvation. Heart-only faith (without confession) is dormant—like electricity that has nothing plugged into it.

Faith in the heart is released through the mouth. There is a connection between inner belief and outward expression, particularly in faith and salvation. Scriptures such as Romans 10:9–10 emphasize that while faith resides in the heart, it's also expressed through confession with the mouth, leading to justification and salvation:

> That if thou shalt confess with thy mouth the Lord Jesus, and shalt believe in thine heart that God hath raised him from the dead, thou shalt be saved. For with the heart man believeth unto righteousness; and with the mouth confession is made unto salvation.

This idea suggests that faith isn't just a silent internal conviction but an outward acknowledgement—lived out through words.

The primary action of biblical faith is speaking—and remaining steadfast in what you've declared. Matthew 17:20 says, "And Jesus said unto them, Because of your unbelief: for verily I say unto you, If ye have faith as a grain of mustard seed, ye shall say unto this mountain, Remove hence to yonder place; and it shall remove; and nothing shall be impossible unto you." Jesus said that if you truly had faith, you would speak it!

Heart-only faith (without confession) is dormant—like electricity that has nothing plugged into it.

Another verse teaches this same principle: "And the Lord said, If ye had faith as a grain of mustard seed, ye might say unto this sycamine tree, Be thou plucked up by the root, and be thou planted in the sea; and it should obey you" (Luke 17:6). Jesus taught about speaking to the sycamine tree. In this profound statement Jesus revealed that faith is not silent. Faith speaks. True faith, even faith as small as a mustard seed, is expressed by speaking with authority and expectation. He used the sycamine tree—known for its deep, stubborn roots—as a metaphor for problems, obstacles, or strongholds that seem immovable. The metaphor teaches a powerful principle: No matter the size of the obstacle, faith is released through words.

Jesus made this principle clear. In Matthew 21:21, He said,

> Verily I say unto you, If ye have faith, and doubt not,
> ye shall not only do this which is done to the fig tree,

but also if ye shall say unto this mountain, Be thou
removed, and be thou cast into the sea; it shall be done.

Jesus was making it clear that what you believe internally
must align with what you say externally for the miraculous to
manifest. What you say is evidence of what you believe. If you
constantly speak fear, worry, and defeat, you're revealing a
heart filled with doubt. If you constantly speak words of hope,
peace, and victory, you're revealing a heart filled with faith.

What you say is evidence of what you believe.
Paul reinforced this concept in
2 Corinthians 4:13: "We also believe,
and therefore speak." Your words
reflect your inner belief system. The
Bible teaches that the mouth is the over-
flow valve of the heart. What resides
deep within your heart—the convictions, fears, doubts, and
hopes—will, over time, find expression through your speech.

Mark 11:23 puts it like this:

> For verily I say unto you, That whosoever shall say
> unto this mountain, Be thou removed, and be thou cast
> into the sea; and shall not doubt in his heart, but shall
> believe that those things which he saith shall come to
> pass; he shall have whatsoever he saith.

Jesus revealed how faith moves mountains. But take note—
Jesus doesn't just talk about believing; He places extraor-
dinary emphasis on saying. As I pointed out before, Jesus
mentioned saying three times in this verse, but He only mentioned believing once. This tells us that while believing in
the heart is essential, speaking with the mouth is what activates and releases faith into the atmosphere.

Words alone are not magic. There must be heart-level

agreement with what you're saying. There needs to be a connection between the words in your mouth and the faith in your heart. Doubt will short-circuit the power of your confession. But if your heart believes and your mouth agrees, nothing will be impossible.

These are the words of Jesus Himself, the author and finisher of our faith. If anyone knows how faith works, it is Jesus. And in Mark 11 He didn't just talk about faith; He demonstrated it, giving us a living example of how to release supernatural power through spoken words. When Peter pointed out the withered fig tree, he was surprised at the power of Jesus' words. But Jesus wasn't surprised. He knew exactly what He was doing. He used this moment to teach them (and us) the spiritual law of faith. The secret Jesus revealed is that faith must be released through words. The lesson learned is that you can have what you say.

Romans 4:17 gives us a divine glimpse into how God operates: "...even God, who quickeneth the dead, and calleth those things which be not as though they were." Two powerful truths are revealed: First, God "quickeneth the dead," meaning God brings life to dead things; and second, He "calleth those things which be not as though they were," meaning God speaks into being what does not yet exist. Faith-filled words bring the dead to life. Faith speaks before it sees. Faith speaks the end from the beginning. Faith-filled words release God's creative power into the earth. Genesis 1 set the precedent. If God creates by speaking and we are made in His image, then our words have the power also to build or destroy, bless or curse, release life or invite death.

Every generation needs to be taught this principle about the power of words. Our children need to learn it. This truth will help shape their futures. They need to be taught the proper way to use their words. Jesus taught something over two thousand years ago, which is still true today: The truth sets us free.

Scripture says that faith is the victory (1 John 5:4). Your words will give you victory. You don't have to live a defeated life. You can win in life. Your words are a key to winning. Your faith and words will help you overcome challenges in life.

Scripture also says that faith is a shield (Eph. 6:16). Your faith can quench all the fiery darts of the enemy. Your words can become a shield. Your words of faith can provide a protective barrier around your life.

Your faith can grow exceedingly. Faith grows by what you hear—even from your own mouth. This is called ever-increasing faith. Keep speaking. Keep confessing. Keep growing in faith. This should become your lifestyle. Speak the Word continually. We live by faith (Gal. 3:11).

You can be strong in faith (Rom. 4:20). Your words will help keep your faith strong. You cannot afford to be weak in this area of your life. Your tongue can release strength.

When the angel appeared to Mary to announce the birth of Jesus, Mary said, "Behold the handmaid of the Lord; be it unto me according to thy word" (Luke 1:38). Mary believed the word of the Lord. Her faith can be seen through her words. Mary agreed with God aloud, and then she received one of the greatest miracles recorded in Scripture. Let your words mirror your faith. Let your confession align with heaven. And watch as God's promises become reality in your life. Don't be like Zacharias, who was struck dumb and could not speak because of his unbelief (Luke 1:20). Although the Word of God can't be thwarted, unbelief often doesn't just stay in our hearts; it comes out of our mouths and affects others and our environment. You need the heart-mouth connection of faith that says, "For with God nothing shall be impossible" (Luke 1:37).

JohnEckhardtBooks.com/chp2

CHAPTER 3

UNLOCK DELIVERANCE

I N THIS CHAPTER we'll cover how the power of your voice can bring deliverance and salvation.

While studying the topic of words, I discovered that each field of study has its own unique set of specialized vocabulary. Aviation professionals, for example, have distinct terminology, just as those in the nautical world—shipping and boating—use words specific to their craft. There is specialized language for computers and technology, engineering, and medicine. Each area relies on its own vocabulary as a way to communicate one's thoughts.

As in the natural so in the Spirit. Did you know that there is a language of the spirit? Not only that, there is inspired language. When you speak by the Spirit of God, you're speaking that language. Heaven has its own language too. And when you begin to speak in heaven's language—speak in God's Word—you'll start to see great breakthroughs and miracles come to pass in your life. What's important to note here is that our words carry a spirit.

Jesus said, "The words that I speak unto you, they are spirit, and they are life" (John 6:63). Words are spiritual containers. They can carry God's Spirit, God's anointing, God's power, and God's wisdom. However, they can also carry something from the enemy: hatred, anger, bitterness, and resentment. You can curse people with your words. Whether they are words of blessing or words of cursing, they are spiritual. When Jesus said, "The words that I speak unto you, they are spirit, and they are life," He was saying that words are spiritual; they release breath, and they release life to you. The Amplified Bible translation of John 6:63 says, "The words I have spoken to you are spirit and life [providing eternal life]." Your words are powerful, and they, of course, are released through your voice, which is why your voice is so powerful. Because your voice is so powerful, the enemy will do anything to stop you from speaking by inspiration—whether that means prophesying, praying, decreeing, singing prophetically, or using your voice to speak life, truth, freedom, victory, and anything else that gets in the way of his plan to steal, kill, and destroy.

Remember, I always teach that when a believer is baptized in the Holy Spirit, God's first act is to take hold of their tongue. Acts 2:4, speaking of the disciples at Pentecost, says, "And they were all filled with the Holy Ghost, and began to speak with other tongues, as the Spirit gave them utterance." Why did the Spirit of God give them that utterance? Because when the Spirit of God moves through your tongue and voice, certain things are released. Scripture says the people heard them "speak in [their] tongues the wonderful works of God" (v. 11). So we can speak God's works. We can give voice to the wonderful works of God—the signs and wonders that God is performing on the earth. We can give voice with praise, with worship, with singing, with preaching, with prophesying, with decree. And once you begin to cause your voice to be released, certain things will begin to happen.

Activate Heaven

I wrote a book called *Activate Heaven*, and it's based on Psalm 19:1, where it says, "The heavens declare the glory of God"—meaning the heavens have a voice. Many times in Scripture, "the heavens" are not referring just to the physical heavens; they're referring to heavenly people. We are heavenly people. We sit in heavenly places. The Spirit of God is the heavenly kingdom, and the kingdom of God is within us. So we speak on heaven's behalf. When you're prophesying, you're speaking as the oracle of God. You're giving voice to heaven. You're causing heaven to be released on earth. "Thy kingdom come, thy will be done on earth, as it is in heaven" (Matt. 6:10). When you start to release heaven, you release healing, deliverance, power, and glory.

When you activate your voice, you're activating heaven. Heaven comes on your behalf. Angels, power, glory, and the hand of God start to manifest. When you speak, you speak as the oracle of God (1 Pet. 4:11). When God speaks through you, when God anoints you to speak, that's heaven speaking. You're activating heaven.

When you activate heaven, you're getting heaven to move on earth. I'm sure you've heard people say phrases such as, "This is a hell on earth," or, "My life is a living hell." But what I'm telling you is that you can have heaven on earth. Rather than saying "I'm living in hell on earth," you can say, "I'm living in heaven on earth." Life on earth can be heaven— the kingdom of God—full of the glory of God. If you're a believer, you can have heaven in your life. No matter what is happening around you, you can have the glory, the presence, and the heaven of God in your life. You can operate your life "as the days of heaven upon earth" (Deut. 11:21). With that in mind, I want to teach you how to use your voice for deliverance.

THE VOICE OF DELIVERANCE

The Book of Romans tells us: "For with the heart man believeth unto righteousness; and with the mouth confession is made unto salvation" (10:10). You believe with your heart, but it is with your mouth—your voice—that confession is made unto salvation. The word for *salvation* in the Greek means deliverance and healing.[1] Salvation is more than just being saved; it is more than going to heaven and not going to hell. It's a word that describes being delivered, restored, healed, and made whole.

When Romans 10:10 says that "with the mouth confession is made unto salvation," it means that with the mouth confession is made unto deliverance. It's interesting that some people want deliverance, but they don't want to change the way they speak. They don't want to get their mouth involved. If you begin to get your mouth involved, your words involved, your voice involved in your life—by speaking the Word of the Lord, speaking faith, speaking by inspiration, and prophesying—you'll begin to see your life change. Because with the mouth confession is made unto salvation, deliverance, and healing, you'll begin to experience miracles, deliverance, healings, and breakthroughs in your life that you've never experienced before.

There is power in your voice to win your battles. There is power in your voice to walk in favor. I want you to grasp just how powerful your voice is—and also how much the enemy wants to stop you from speaking. He wants to stop you from moving in faith and moving in the prophetic. This is why I preach on the prophetic so much. The prophetic—or prophecy—is inspired utterance. When you prophesy and speak as the oracle of God, your life will change because you're releasing your voice. The words you speak will be spirit, and there will be life. Get your voice involved in your life. Confess the Word of God, prophesy, and speak as the oracle of God.

Allow the Spirit of God to drop His Word in your tongue and speak. Don't be afraid. Don't shut down. Don't allow the enemy to destroy your life because you say nothing. No! Rise up. Release your voice. Release your words. It's good when others speak over you and bless you, but there are times when you need to release your own voice.

God has given you a voice for a reason. One of the most amazing things you have is your voice. God has given you a unique voice that no one else has. It's like a fingerprint. God hears your voice. God responds to your voice. The angel told Daniel, "I have come because of your words" (Dan. 10:12, ESV). The angel came because of Daniel's words. From the first day Daniel began to pray—at the moment Daniel's voice was heard in heaven—the angel was released. It took the angel twenty-one days to break through and overcome the enemy blocking him, but he kept coming because of Daniel's words.

God has given you a unique voice that no one else has. It's like a fingerprint.

God shows up because of your words—because of your voice. Whether you're singing, praying, crying out, calling out, or prophesying, God responds to your voice. This revelation can change your life. Amid troubles, darkness, pain, frustration, discouragement, or depression, lift your voice, open your mouth, and begin to decree and speak. Remember, as we looked at in Mark 11:23, faith believes *and* speaks:

> That whosoever shall say unto this mountain, Be thou removed, and be thou cast into the sea; and shall not doubt in his heart, but shall believe that those things which he saith shall come to pass; he shall have whatsoever he saith.

I know some people say, "Well, I don't believe in all that saying and having it or blabbing and grabbing it." Well, those people have an issue with Jesus because that's what He said. That's the Word of the Lord. If Jesus said it, you can believe it. "With the mouth confession is made unto salvation" (Rom. 10:10). If you need deliverance and breakthroughs, open your mouth, speak, and decree. The power of words, the power of our voices, is why I do so many decrees. For example, I decree over the finances of people, and their finances start to change. People say, "Well, you have to work." I understand that you have to work. But you first have to believe God for your finances. I'm not saying you just make a decree over your finances and then sit on your couch, waiting for money to miraculously appear. I'm not saying to declare something and then don't do anything. I am saying that the very act of saying it is important because Jesus said, "The words that I speak unto you, they are spirit" (John 6:63).

Your voice is powerful. Your voice is the voice of deliverance.

Words affect the spirit realm. They are spirit, and they are life. Even though you hear the words in the natural, there's a spirit behind the words you say. If you're speaking as the oracle of God, you're giving voice to the Word of the Lord. You're putting the Word of God in your mouth.

I want to encourage you to open your mouth. When you start to decree, speak, prophesy, sing, and release your words, you'll be walking in great deliverance and breakthroughs. Your voice is powerful. Your voice is the voice of healing. Your voice is the voice of salvation. Your voice is the voice of deliverance.

WORDS OF DELIVERANCE

Words carry power. Words can bring deliverance. Matthew 8:16 says, "When the even was come, they brought unto him many that were possessed with devils: and he cast out the spirits with his word, and healed all that were sick." Jesus cast out devils with words. His words carried power. His words brought deliverance. His words were spoken with authority, and the demons obeyed.

You have authority too. You have been given the keys of the kingdom (Matt. 16:19). This gives you the authority to bind and loose. Keys represent the authority to lock (or bind) or unlock (or loose). Believers must know and operate in authority. Jesus gave His disciples power and authority over all devils (Matt. 10:1). We are seated with Christ in heavenly places far above all principality and powers (Eph. 1:20; 2:6).

Your words can and should be spoken with authority. Demons will obey your words. Words are a key to breakthroughs and miracles. You can command with your words. Many believers suffer unnecessarily because they fail to exercise their authority and use their voices to speak words of deliverance.

One of the ways we can speak words of deliverance is through renunciation. Second Corinthians 4:2 says,

> But have renounced the hidden things of dishonesty, not walking in craftiness, nor handling the word of God deceitfully; but by manifestation of the truth commending ourselves to every man's conscience in the sight of God.

You can renounce things with your words. Renunciation is a key to freedom and deliverance. I have applied this truth in the ministry of deliverance. Many experienced freedom after they renounced things with their words. The word *renounce* is defined as formally declaring one's abandonment of something bad or evil. Renunciation with words will break any right or claim of the enemy in your life. You can renounce sins, habits, relationships, organizations, false teachings, and ungodly lifestyles with words.

Sometimes, to help people experience deliverance, we instruct them to renounce things aloud in their own words. Here are some examples of renunciations:

- I renounce all hatred, anger, resentment, revenge, retaliation, unforgiveness, and bitterness in the name of Jesus.

- I renounce all lust, perversion, immorality, uncleanness, impurity, and sexual sin in the name of Jesus.

- I renounce all pride, haughtiness, arrogance, vanity, ego, disobedience, and rebellion in the name of Jesus.

- I renounce all fear, unbelief, and doubt in the name of Jesus.

When we are doing deliverance ministry, we guide them to say the renunciation. When they say it, chains break, and demons manifest because they chose to speak up. Deliverance happens because they use their authority and their words to initiate the decreeing process. Sometimes when I pray for people, I take them through prayers of repentance and renunciation. I have them say them aloud. The enemy will occasionally come up and try to choke them to stop them from saying these prayers. Once they complete the renunciation, the enemy knows breakthroughs and miracles will happen in their lives. He knows that once they open their mouths and speak words that are filled with spirit and life, deliverance will inevitably come.

Repentance is enacted with words. Repentance is another way we can speak words of deliverance. Hosea 14:2 says, "Take with you words, and turn to the LORD: say unto him, Take away all iniquity, and receive us graciously: so will we render the calves of our lips." Another translation says, "Take words of repentance with you and return to the LORD" (csb). The prodigal son returned home with words. He confessed his sin to his father, and he was received with open arms (Luke 15:18–21). Words of repentance can also lead to restoration. David's words of repentance are recorded in Psalm 51. He was forgiven and restored. Words are powerful.

We can also speak words of deliverance through prayer. Prayer is a powerful weapon against the enemy. A prayer of deliverance can be as simple as, "Keep my soul, and deliver me." (See Psalm 25:20.) Here are some other prayers of deliverance:

Make haste, O God, and deliver me (Ps. 70:1).

Deliver me, O God, out of the hand of the enemy (Ps. 71:4).

Deliver me from all my fears (Ps. 34:4).

Deliver me from evil (Matt. 6:13).

Let evil spirits be cast out (Acts 19:12).

I put on the whole armor of God that I might stand in the evil day (Eph. 6:13).

Give Your angels charge over me, and deliver me (Ps. 91:11).

I have the keys of the kingdom, and whatever I bind on earth is bound in heaven, and whatever I loose on earth is loosed in heaven (Matt. 16:19).

I loose myself from the bands of wickedness (Isa. 58:6).

DELIVERANCE FROM ATTACKS AGAINST YOUR VOICE

If you have lost your voice—not just naturally but spiritually—you need to pray. The enemy has come against you and taken away your voice. It seems as if you have nothing to say or you don't want to speak anymore. You're discouraged; you're frustrated; you're depressed. If this sounds like you, I pray that you will regain your voice, that your voice will be restored, that you will speak words of power, and that you will walk in miracles, power, and salvation.

I want you to put your hand on your voice box and read these decrees aloud:

In the name of Jesus, there's a new anointing coming on my voice and words.

I receive a fresh anointing to speak as the oracle of God.

From this day forward, when I open my mouth, I believe miracles will be released. Every time I open my mouth, I expect a miracle.

Your finances are about to change. Your mind is about to change. Your family is about to change. Your ministry is about to change. You will prophesy to your city or your nation, and the government and economy will change because you opened your mouth and decreed it.

The Lord is saying that your voice is about to change things.

Now, pray:

Lord, thank You for releasing my voice. Every demon that has come against my voice, I rebuke you in the name of Jesus. You cannot kill my voice. You cannot stop my voice. You cannot hinder my voice. Every spirit that has attacked my voice, I rebuke you. My voice is loosed in the name of Jesus. Amen.

JohnEckhardtBooks.com/chp3

CHAPTER 4

THE ABUNDANCE
OF THE HEART

W E ARE WRITING words on our hearts when we speak. Psalm 45:1 says, "My heart is inditing a good matter: I speak of the things which I have made touching the king: my tongue is the pen of a ready writer." Our hearts are tablets. Write good things on your heart—for out of the abundance of the heart the mouth speaks (Matt. 12:34). It's the cycle we talked about with the heart-mouth connection. When you speak the Word of God—when you speak words of faith—you are not only speaking but also hearing those words. Since faith comes by hearing, speaking the Word of God inscribes those words once again on your heart and allows the cycle to continue.

FROM THE ABUNDANCE OF THE HEART

The tongue reveals the heart. Jesus said,

> A good man out of the good treasure of his heart bringeth forth that which is good; and an evil man out of the evil treasure of his heart bringeth forth that which

is evil: for of the abundance of the heart his mouth
speaketh.

—Luke 6:45

Whatever is in your heart in abundance will come out of
your mouth. That is why you must guard your heart.

The issues of your life come out of your heart and proceed
through your words. Proverbs 4:23 says, "Keep thy heart
with all diligence; for out of it are the issues of life." What
comes out of your heart sets the course of your life. The
Pharisees could not speak good things because their hearts
were evil. They were filled with pride and envy. Their words
revealed their hearts.

You must be diligent in guarding both your heart and your
words because they are connected. Your heart is the source
of your life. Your life and future spring from it. Your heart is
a fountain from which your words spring
forth. Your heart can be a fountain of life.
Your words can be filled with life.

What comes out of your heart sets the course of your life.

It is also true that what comes out of
your mouth can defile you. Jesus said,
"Not that which goeth into the mouth
defileth a man; but that which cometh out
of the mouth, this defileth a man" (Matt. 15:11).

The Bible clearly warns against corrupt and perverse
speech coming out of your mouth from your heart: "Put away
from thee a froward mouth, and perverse lips put far from
thee" (Prov. 4:24). Perverse speech refers to twisted, morally
corrupt words—profane, vulgar, or rebellious language. The
amount of vulgarity that is spoken today is beyond belief.
We are commanded to keep evil talk away from our lips.

What is your tongue worth? Proverbs 10:20 says, "The

tongue of the just is as choice silver: the heart of the wicked is little worth." Your tongue can be as choice silver. Choice silver is precious and of great value. Do your words have value? Are your words worth speaking? Your words should not be worthless. In Scripture, speaking worthless or idle words implies speaking carelessly or frivolously, especially in a way that is unhelpful or lacks substance. Jesus said, "Moreover, I tell you this: on the Day of Judgment people will have to give account for every careless word they have spoken" (Matt. 12:36, CJB). This is a sobering scripture when it comes to words.

Your words matter, and when worthless, idle, corrupt, or perverse words are coming out of your mouth, it indicates a heart-related issue that needs to be addressed.

LIFE AND DEATH ARE IN THE POWER OF THE TONGUE

Good things are connected with your mouth. If you want good things to happen, you have to speak correctly. Psalm 34:12 says, "What man is he that desireth life, and loveth many days, that he may see good?" Doesn't everyone want to have life and live many days and see good? In other words, it's not just about living many days, but it's about living many days and seeing good as you live a long life. We don't want to live a long life filled with bad things. We want to live a long life filled with good things.

Well, the key to living a good, long life is found in the next verses of Psalm 34: "Keep thy tongue from evil, and thy lips from speaking guile. Depart from evil, and do good; seek peace, and pursue it" (vv. 13–14). Keep your tongue from evil. Keep your lips from speaking hypocritically or speaking deceitfully. Depart from evil; do good. Seek and pursue peace, or shalom. These are the keys to having a long, good life.

Many people don't understand the destructive cycles caused by bad speaking. Proverbs 18:21 says, "Death and life are in the power of the tongue." Your tongue is what governs your life. Acts, chapter 2, says that when the Spirit of God came onto the disciples, they "began to speak with other tongues, as the Spirit gave them utterance" (v. 4). The Spirit of God anointed and inspired them to speak in other languages—in other tongues. Why? Because if the Holy Spirit can control your tongue, He controls your life.

The Apostle James wrote,

> Behold, we put bits in the horses' mouths, that they may obey us; and we turn about their whole body. Behold also the ships, which though they be so great, and are driven of fierce winds, yet are they turned about with a very small helm, whithersoever the governor listeth. Even so the tongue is a little member, and boasteth great things. Behold, how great a matter a little fire kindleth!
>
> —JAMES 3:3–5

James was saying that just like a small bridle controls a horse and a small rudder controls a ship, your tongue—even though it is small—controls your life. The words you speak are powerful: "A man shall eat good by the fruit of his mouth" (Prov. 13:2). What is in your heart comes out of your mouth and affects your life—for good or evil. Death and life are in the power of the tongue (Prov. 18:21).

You can decree things, and it's established unto you. Job 22:28 says, "Thou shalt also decree a thing, and it shall be established unto thee." This is a reason the prophetic is so important. When you prophesy, you speak by the inspiration of God. Those prophetic words don't just give information; they cause things to be established, aligned, changed, and shifted. They set the course for your life.

When you make confessions, speak words of life, and set your course by the words of your mouth, you will see changes in your life. But you cannot speak words of death and decree evil and then expect to have a long, good life. You cannot lie, gossip, backbite, criticize, and slander—even behind the scenes—and expect good things to come into your life. Good things are connected to your tongue, so keep your tongue from speaking evil. Guard your mouth. Watch what you say. Do not allow your tongue to be used against people. Do not be critical. Do not operate in jealousy and envy and hatred with your words.

It amazes me how people expect their lives to change, but they don't think to govern their tongues. You have to govern your tongue, which means you also have to govern your heart, because from the abundance of the heart the mouth speaks (Luke 6:45). When your heart is right, when you get bitterness, envy, jealousy, pride, and anger out of your heart, and when you cleanse your heart with the Word of God, it will be reflected in your words.

> *It amazes me how people expect their lives to change, but they don't think to govern their tongues.*

Jesus told the religious leaders of His day, "O generation of vipers, how can ye, being evil, speak good things?" (Matt. 12:34). You can't speak good things from an evil heart. It's impossible. Jesus also said, "Even so every good tree bringeth forth good fruit; but a corrupt tree bringeth forth evil fruit. A good tree cannot bring forth evil fruit, neither can a corrupt tree bring forth good fruit" (Matt. 7:17–18). A good tree has a good root system and brings forth good fruit. A good person with a good heart will bring forth good words.

You can always tell what the hearts of people are like by the words that are coming out of their mouths. What they say is an indicator of what is in their hearts. So if you want good things, you have to change your confession. You have to guard your tongue. You have to guard your heart and keep it with all diligence. If you show me someone who doesn't guard their tongue, I'll show you someone who has many bad days and doesn't see good things come their way. But if you show me someone who watches their words, guards their heart, speaks kindly of others, confesses good things, uses words that impart life, and honors and blesses people, I'll show you someone who has good things come continually their way.

KNOW WHO YOU ARE

You need to know who you are. You need to know what purposes and plans God put specifically in your heart. It is so important that you understand this, because the devil will try to make you think you are not special, that you are just another person here trying to make it. You aren't. The kingdom of God, which is heaven, resides in you. The problems we experience so often boil down to the fact that we don't know our identity in Christ. We don't know who we are. We don't understand the things God has placed in our hearts. We don't know what happens when we open our mouths. We don't know what happens when we sing about the anointing of God. We don't understand what happens when we prophesy. We can become so accustomed to these spiritual activities that we just take them for granted, and we forget the power we have in our voices.

The devil uses this and tries to put a muzzle on our mouths. He tries to make us think we can't say anything, or if we do, it won't make a difference. But I pray that if you come close to shutting up, you'll feel like Jeremiah—as if there is fire shut up in your bones: "If I say, 'I will not mention his word or speak anymore in his name,' his word is in my heart like a fire, a fire shut up in my bones. I am weary of holding it in; indeed, I cannot" (Jer. 20:9, NIV).

Every person or circumstance that the enemy used to silence you must not have known that you can't shut up heaven. The devices of the enemy that tried to limit your voice—by suggesting that your voice is not important, that you can't go far, or that you are limited to preaching a small sermon to a small group—do not know the power of heaven in your voice.

What's happening now—with some not-so-good aspects—is that everyone has a phone and their own "TV" program through Facebook Live, Instagram Live, YouTube, or any of many other streaming platforms. There is no reason for any of us to remain silent when God has put a word in our mouths. Nor is there reason to stay silent when the Word of God, written on our hearts, is ready to come forth through the heart-mouth connection.

Each of us speaks with our different gifts and graces. We're not the same. Two apostles can be different. Two prophets can be different. Don't try to be like someone else. Be who God has called you to be. Do what God has called you to do. Go where He sends you. Don't be a copycat. Don't be a clone. It's OK to receive an impartation from someone, but God has created you to be unique. Don't be born an original and die a copy. We have too many copies out here. You need to write the Word of God on your heart and be exactly who God has called *you* to be.

When you walk in a special grace, anointing, ability, or talent, it opens you up to the realm of what I call the realm of special miracles—a distinct class of miracles. Evidence for this can be found in Acts 19:11, which says, "And God wrought special miracles by the hands of Paul." This passage tells us that there is a miracle realm, and then there is a special miracle realm. The word *special* simply means something unusual, something better, or something on a higher level. In the New King James Version, the same verse says, "Now God worked *unusual* miracles by the hands of Paul" (emphasis added).

As you walk in your new heavenly identity, you need to understand how important it is that the Lord performs special miracles for you and through you. This is how you demonstrate the things of heaven that can be loosed in others' lives. It is also how God will bless you, so that by your words and actions, the special miracles of heaven will be released into the lives of those God sends you.

For you and through you, God wants to do something different—something unusual. He wants to perform some unusual miracles, open some unusual doors, bring unusual breakthroughs, raise you to unusual levels, and create unusual connections. God wants to do something unusual for you and through you.

In studying the word *special*, you will find that it is not a word frequently used in the King James Version. It is used more often in other translations such as the Amplified Bible, the Voice translation, the Passion Translation, and the Living

Bible. If you study how the word is used, you will see it show up in the phrase "special messenger" (e.g., Rom. 1:1, AMP)—the apostles were called special messengers. There is also a reference to "special endowments," where the word "special" is used to describe an unusual impartation of the gifts of the Spirit (1 Cor. 12:1, AMP). The Apostle Peter wrote about this concept:

> As each of you has received a gift (a particular spiritual talent, a gracious divine endowment), employ it for one another as [befits] good trustees of God's many-sided grace [faithful stewards of the extremely diverse powers and gifts granted to Christians by unmerited favor].
> —1 PETER 4:10, AMPC

Spirit-filled ministry—especially prophecy and the laying on of hands—is a vehicle through which gifts or special endowments are released into your life. The Apostle Paul instructed Timothy to stir up the gift, or special endowment, that was given to him through prophecy with the laying on of hands by the presbytery:

> Do not neglect the gift which is in you, [that special inward endowment] which was directly imparted to you [by the Holy Spirit] by prophetic utterance when the elders laid their hands upon you [at your ordination].
> —1 TIMOTHY 4:14, AMPC

Paul again told Timothy in 2 Timothy 1:6 not to neglect the gift God had given him through the laying on of his hands.

Special endowments come directly from God through the laying on of hands in prophecy. These are unique gifts: prophecy, tongues, interpretation of tongues, faith, gifts of healing, the working of miracles, word of knowledge, word of wisdom, discerning of spirits, mercy, giving, exhortation, serving, and others. (See Romans 12.) All of these special endowments are connected to the miraculous—when you move in words of knowledge, words of wisdom, and discerning of spirits; and when you prophesy, speak in tongues, or interpret tongues, miracles are released. These gifts are imparted as special abilities to individuals with special assignments, commissions, or mandates.

The Apostle Paul had a special commission to preach to the Gentiles. One of the places he went—Macedonia—became known to him through a dream. To help Paul carry out the mission God assigned him, God gave him an endowment of special miracles. You're reading this because God has placed a special calling in your heart and given you a unique assignment—a place where your voice will have great impact. This doesn't necessarily mean God is calling you to a worldwide platform; your assignment is something special. It may be in the local church, the marketplace, politics, or media. Whether your assignment is local, national, or international, it is a special one. God has given you a unique heart, a unique voice, and a unique way to activate heaven. He has imparted to you a special vision and a special gift. What God has placed within your heart is unique, different, and sets you apart from others.

RISE, SHINE, AND COME FORTH

Some time ago I was leading a congregation through a series of prophetic activations. During one activation, we encouraged people to listen for the sound of the Lord. When you are tuned into the Spirit in this way, the Lord may give you sounds—wind blowing, rain falling, birds singing, or even trains. On this occasion I heard the sound of an army marching; in the spirit, I heard boots marching. Then the Lord gave me a verse in Psalm 68: "The Lord gave the word: great was the company of those that published it" (v. 11).

The Hebrew word *sābā'* is translated as company, which means "army."[1] It is also rendered as "an army of women" in some Bible versions (e.g., MEV). Somehow the King James Version left that part out. Some people don't think women can preach or prophesy, but every married man knows women preach.

As I was leading this activation, I began to see the need for revival and breakthrough in America. There is so much happening in our country—perversion, rebellion, witchcraft, violence, hatred, and injustice. It's amazing. Yet I believe that when it is darkest, prophetic people rise.

Elijah was the prophet during Jezebel's rule over the nation. Two of the most wicked people ever to ascend the throne—Ahab and Jezebel—were in control, but God raised up Elijah. God has a way of raising up strong anointings when the world seems dark, when it appears the devil is taking over and witchcraft is prevailing. The strongest anointings arise when conditions are dire. Strong people are raised up who know how to pray and fast, preach and teach—people who know how to rebuke, take authority, and prophesy.

When it is darkest, prophetic people rise.

No matter how dark things become, the Bible still says, "Arise, shine; for thy light is come, and the glory of the LORD is risen upon thee. For, behold, the darkness shall cover the earth, and gross darkness the people: but the LORD shall arise upon thee, and his glory shall be seen upon thee" (Isa. 60:1–2).

When darkness tries to cover the land, it is time for you to obey what God puts in your heart—it is time for you to shine, rise, and come forth. God is raising up a new breed of believers who will prophesy, pray, preach, teach, bind, and loose. He is raising up an army that understands the power of words, a company of people who know that no weapon formed against them shall prosper. When the enemy comes in like a flood, the Spirit of the Lord will raise a standard against him (Isa. 59:19).

No matter how bad things become, one word can turn a situation around. All it takes is one word from God to change everything. This concept of being a voice, activating heavens, or having a voice that moves heaven is not simply about people declaring, "Thus saith the Lord." It is about an army of believers God is raising up—an army into whose hearts and mouths God will put His word so that when they release it, something will shake and change.

Things are changing politically, and division is widespread, particularly in America. It seems as if everybody hates everybody. We have problems with people in the military, the police department, authority, racism, prejudice, Democrats versus Republicans, and drugs. Since the COVID-19 pandemic, many things have come undone and need to be set back in order. Yet I believe God will send people with His words in their hearts and in their mouths—with solutions, skill, wisdom, and insight—and we will see that the best is yet to come.

Lord, let us keep our tongues from evil and our lips
from speaking guile. Grant us long life and many

good days. Let good things come to us. Let us enjoy good things by the fruit of our mouths. Father, I pray that this word will give everyone a revelation of their part in seeing good things come. God will give us good things, but we have a part to play. Lord, thank You that my tongue is submitted to Your Spirit. My tongue is the pen of a ready writer. My tongue will praise You and glorify You. I will put the Word of God in my mouth, confess Your Word, and prophesy. I will speak by the inspiration of God. I will avoid gossip, slander, backbiting, profanity, ungodly speech, and evil speaking. I will not listen to or participate in such things because, God, I want good things to come my way.

JohnEckhardtBooks.com/chp4

CHAPTER 5

TAMING THE TONGUE

I T SEEMS AS though many in the body of Christ have embraced the belief that no one has the right to judge anybody. Some say everyone sins every day. Such thinking is used to excuse both the body of Christ and its leaders, but it is a lie from the enemy. You can live right. You can live virtuously. You can bear the fruit of the Spirit. You can live in love and humility. If you are sinning every day, then you are not saved. I understand that anyone can make a mistake, but it shouldn't be habitual. We often hear believers say, "We are sinners. We all sin. Therefore, we can't judge anybody." But Scripture says, "He that committeth sin is of the devil; for the devil sinneth from the beginning. For this purpose the Son of God was manifested, that he might destroy the works of the devil" (1 John 3:8).

Anyone can make a mistake, but it shouldn't be habitual.

Don't buy into the lie that no one can live righteously. The whole purpose of salvation is to give us victory over sin and reconnect us to God so that, through the power of the Spirit of God, we may be holy as He is holy. Anybody can

THE POWER OF YOUR WORDS

THE POWER OF YOUR WORDS

have a bad day. But you shouldn't have 364 of them—especially if the only day you didn't sin was the day you slept all day.

No, God wants to set us free from the religious mindset that all of us are sinners. That mindset loves to put everyone in the same boat—as if "everyone is a sinner" were our center and standard. Such people want to put everyone on the same level as themselves, which allows them to excuse cursing, lying, gossiping, and lusting. For some it may seem impossible to abstain from these actions, but with God it is possible to live purely and with virtue.

This is why the Lord showed me that we should add to our faith, virtue, and then to our virtue, knowledge (2 Pet. 1:5). Virtue must come first, before delving into all the deep things. Don't be so eager for knowledge that you skip over virtue.

Having knowledge without virtue means your life will be open to certain things, and you may find yourself caught up in habitual sin and unholy behaviors. Your lifestyle will not be virtuous enough to sustain you. You can have a great singing voice, write books, preach the house down, and be in a high position with all kinds of titles, yet be proud, arrogant, and rude. You can go to seminary, have all the revelation, know all the Hebrew, and be ordained, yet abuse and manipulate others. You can find yourself in whatever pulpit or marketplace position that is open to you, "preaching" your message your way, and have no virtue, no purity, no righteousness, and no representation of the character of God.

VOICE AND VIRTUE

Some time ago I'd been studying the word *chayil*. It's a Hebrew word that translates to the English word "virtuous" in Proverbs 31:10. Because this word carries so much significance and is used throughout the Old and New Testaments,

I wrote a book about it called *Chayil: Release the Power of a Virtuous Woman.* We even hosted a conference by the same name. As I have already written and spoken about on many occasions, the Lord impressed on me the significance of this word *virtuous*, which means power, strength, moral excellence, and good character.

While I had focused on the Bible translations that reflected the power-related meanings for the word, the Lord said to me, "You cannot walk in the power aspects of the chayil anointing without also having virtue." By this He meant possessing moral excellence and good character. Then the Lord gave me a scripture from 2 Peter. The passage shook me, because it showed He was challenging me in this area:

> Whereby are given unto us exceeding great and precious promises: that by these ye might be partakers of the divine nature, having escaped the corruption that is in the world through lust. And beside this, giving all diligence, add to your faith virtue; and to virtue knowledge; and to knowledge temperance; and to temperance patience; and to patience godliness; and to godliness brotherly kindness; and to brotherly kindness charity.
>
> —2 Peter 1:4–7

When I read this verse, the Lord said to me, "Notice the first thing I do: I tell My people to add to their faith not knowledge but virtue." Then He continued, "A lot of believers—when they get saved—have faith, but instead of virtue, the first thing they want to add to their lives is knowledge."

Whenever we come into something new—a new job; a new assignment; a new place; a new discovery about ourselves, such as a gift or personality trait; a new prophetic word—we start reading books, signing up for training or coaching, seeking mentorship, or attending conferences. These are all things that give us knowledge. But we often skip over virtue.

The 1828 edition of Webster's Dictionary defines *virtue* as "bravery, valor," which was "the predominant signification of virtus among the Romans." It also notes that "this sense is nearly or quite obsolete." Another definition of *virtue* is "moral goodness; the practice of moral duties and the abstaining from vice, or a conformity of life and conversation to the moral law. In this sense, *virtue* may be, and in many instances must be, distinguished from religion. The practice of moral duties merely from motives of convenience, or from compulsion, or from regard to reputation, is *virtue* as distinct from religion. The practice of moral duties from sincere love to God and his laws, is *virtue* and religion."[1]

A virtuous life is in sync with God's holy standards.

In the same vein, author and minister Art Katz says that perhaps virtue is "an archaic word, used in the times of the King James translators as a synonym for power, but today the word *virtue* has to do with things ethical and moral."[2] He is speaking to how the word's definition, understanding, and usage have changed over time. Like Katz I believe the various uses of this word are "more than just an accident of time and language." There is "a conjunction between virtue and power...the amount of power for healing [and the myriads of other gifts], in us as in Him, is relative to the proportion of virtue [ethical and moral excellence] in which we walk."[3]

A virtuous life is in sync with God's holy standards. A preacher once put it like this: "Virtue is the Godly influence of a life that is in a right relationship with the Lord and filled with the power of the Holy Spirit."[4]

Synonyms for virtue that shed more light on it being about living according to moral and ethical standards are "character, decency, goodness, honesty, integrity, morality, probity, rectitude, righteousness, rightness, uprightness."[5]

Then when we go to the Word, we see where virtue is joined with righteousness, morality, and justice.

> For the LORD is [absolutely] righteous, He loves righteousness (virtue, morality, justice); the upright shall see His face.
>
> —PSALM 11:7, AMP

Jesus loved virtue. He was anointed with the oil of gladness because of virtue.

> You have loved righteousness (virtue, morality, justice) and hated wickedness; therefore God, your God, has anointed You above Your companions with the oil of jubilation.
>
> —PSALM 45:7, AMP

Virtue is integrity and uprightness in purpose. Lawlessness and injustice are the opposites of virtue.

> You have loved righteousness [integrity, virtue, uprightness in purpose] and have hated lawlessness [injustice, sin]. Therefore God, Your God, has anointed You with the oil of gladness above Your companions.
>
> —HEBREWS 1:9, AMP

Wisdom admonishes us to hold on to the virtues of loyalty and kindness.

Never tire of loyalty and kindness. Hold these virtues
tightly. Write them deep within your heart.

—PROVERBS 3:3, TLB

Paul lists virtues we should have as God's chosen people.
These virtues include compassion, kindness, humility, gentleness, patience, forgiveness, and love.

Therefore, as God's chosen people, holy and dearly
loved, clothe yourselves with compassion, kindness,
humility, gentleness and patience. Bear with each other
and forgive one another if any of you has a grievance
against someone. Forgive as the Lord forgave you. And
over all these virtues put on love, which binds them all
together in perfect unity.

—COLOSSIANS 3:12–14, NIV

Having virtue is also about honesty.

My hope is in you, so may goodness [blamelessness;
innocence] and honesty [virtue] guard me.

—PSALM 25:21, EXB

Those who are honest [have integrity/virtue] will live
in the land, and those who are innocent [blameless]
will remain in it.

—PROVERBS 2:21, EXB

Virtue gives you the ability to live a good life.

People who live good lives [walk in virtue/integrity]
respect [fear] the LORD, but those who live evil lives
don't [go the wrong way on their paths despise him].

—PROVERBS 14:2, EXB

When people try to rush past the process and want to skip over cultivating the traits in life that produce good character and moral excellence, we end up with people who gain a lot of knowledge but have no character to sustain the promotion God brings into their lives. In prophetic and Spirit-filled circles they may learn all about the prophetic, the apostolic, deliverance, and spiritual warfare, and in the wider church they may learn about giving, faith, and prayer, but they skip virtue. Even many ministers have a lot of knowledge but lack virtue.

Trying to amplify your voice before you have obtained virtue is a fall waiting to happen.

This is dangerous and does not work when it comes to using your voice in a way that moves heaven. The main reason this doesn't work is because knowledge puffs up (1 Cor. 8:1). Knowledge without virtue can lead to pride, and God resists the proud (Jas. 4:6). Their voices may sound good to those who are hearing with their natural ears, but in the spirit, their sound will have little effect—it will be like tinkling brass and a sounding cymbal. But it is the prayers of the righteous (or virtuous) that avail much (Jas. 5:16). It is to the humble that God grants His grace. Trying to use and amplify your voice before you have obtained virtue is a fall waiting to happen.

Nowadays, in some circles, everybody knows about the apostolic and prophetic. You go on social media, and everyone is an apostle or prophet. Everyone is treating Facebook Live as if it's a TV program. It's so easy to take the little you know, get your phone, and go live on social media. If someone comes on your broadcast from overseas, you now have an international ministry.

People like these get a little knowledge in a certain area and are ready for God to send them to the nations, promote them, and make their name and face known, but they have no virtue. They can operate in power and have all the knowledge of how to cast out devils, heal the sick, and prophesy, but their character is flawed.

Virtue has the power to make a person whole. Virtue is a life force that flows from Christ. The woman who touched Jesus in Luke 8 was made whole and was told to go in peace. The power Jesus had that healed the sick is called virtue. Jesus felt virtue leave His body. This indicates that virtue can be measured. Multitudes were healed and made whole through the virtue that flowed from Christ. There was enough virtue in Christ to heal them all (Luke 9:11).

Virtue can produce miracles since it can cause you to be holy. The virtue in Christ—both in power and in character—can be accessed by faith. Faith, therefore, is a conduit through which virtue flows. You can use your faith to receive virtue from the Lord.

DON'T BE HUNG BY YOUR TONGUE

Lack of virtue will limit your voice. Virtue doesn't just refer to your actions; it covers your words. As Francis Martin's book title says, don't be "hung by the tongue."[6]

Don't let your tongue hang you. Don't let your tongue bring death and destruction into your life. Don't kill yourself by your words. The foundational scripture I have already mentioned is Proverbs 18:21: "Death and life are in the power of the tongue: and they that love it shall eat the fruit thereof."

You eat the fruit of what you say. Death and life are in the power of the tongue. You can speak death, or you can speak life. Your tongue is a creative force that can produce life or death. Words are not just sounds; they carry power. Words shape your world. You eat the fruit of what you say, good or bad. You are either hung by the tongue or helped by it. So ask yourself, "What kind of words am I speaking daily? Do I speak more life or more death?"

God created the universe by speaking, and we are made in His image: "And God said, Let us make man in our image, after our likeness" (Gen. 1:26). Because we are made in God's image, we can speak like Him. Because we are made in God's image, our words carry power. Hebrews 11:3 says, "Through faith we understand that the worlds were framed by the word of God." As God framed the world with words, so we also frame our lives with our words.

Let me say that again: We frame our lives with our words. God didn't think the world into existence—He spoke it. That's the principle of Genesis 1: God said…God said…God said.

Jesus said,

> Have faith in God. For verily I say unto you, That whosoever shall say unto this mountain, Be thou removed, and be thou cast into the sea; and shall not doubt in his heart, but shall believe that those things which he saith shall come to pass; he shall have whatsoever he saith.
>
> —MARK 11:22–23

We must believe and speak. That's the faith principle I mentioned earlier. Stop declaring what you see, what you feel, or what you fear. Declare what you believe.

Words reveal your heart. If faith is in your heart, faith comes out of your mouth. If fear is in your heart, fear comes out of your mouth. If bitterness is in your heart, bitterness comes out of your mouth. If anger, criticism, or pride is in your heart, that's what comes out of your mouth. As we have already learned, out of the abundance of the heart the mouth speaks (Matt. 12:34). So if you have the Word of God in abundance, if you have faith in abundance, if you have love in abundance, that is what will come out of your mouth.

Your words are a mirror of your heart. If you want to change your words, you must first change what's in your heart. James 3:10 says, "Out of the same mouth proceedeth blessing and cursing. My brethren, these things ought not so to be." The way you change what's in your heart is through repentance, asking God to cleanse you.

If you want to change your words, you must first change what's in your heart.

Jeremiah 17:9 says, "The heart is deceitful above all things, and desperately wicked: who can know it?" That is an old-covenant scripture that talks about a heart that has not been regenerated. But under the new covenant, you can have a different kind of heart. As a matter of fact, in the new covenant, when you repent and accept Christ, God gives you a new heart: "Therefore if any man be in Christ, he is a new creature: old things are passed away; behold, all things are become new" (2 Cor. 5:17). You don't have the same sinful, evil heart. You get a new heart, cleansed of all your sin.

Once God gives you a new heart, it is no longer desperately wicked. But you need to keep it clean: "Keep thy heart with all diligence; for out of it are the issues of life" (Prov. 4:23). Keep your heart. Guard your heart. Put a fence around your heart. Don't let anything such as doubt, unbelief, unforgiveness, bitterness, lust, anger, or hatred take root in your heart. Don't let them in your heart, because what's in your heart will come out of your mouth, and what comes out of your mouth will shape your world, your future, and your destiny. You can't hide bitterness, unbelief, or fear for long. They will come out in your speech, even if it's unconsciously done. You speak things because they're in your heart. They're in the inner man, the hidden man of the heart.

Instead of allowing sin to take root in your heart, put the Word in your heart by putting it in your mouth. Romans 10:8 says, "The word is nigh thee, even in thy mouth, and in thy heart." It's that heart-mouth connection again. When you put the Word in your heart, it comes out of your mouth. And when you put the Word in your mouth, it gets in your heart. Why? Because "faith cometh by hearing, and hearing by the word of God" (Rom. 10:17). Put the Word in your mouth, and reprogram your heart. If you've allowed doubt or unbelief in your heart, repent of it and be delivered from it. Ask God to renew and cleanse your heart and then speak the Word of God over your heart.

Spend time meditating on God's Word to fill your heart with faith and hope. Fill your heart with words of faith instead of words of fear. The story of the twelve spies sent to check out the Promised Land demonstrates the difference between words of faith and words of fear. Caleb spoke words of faith: "Let us go up at once, and possess it; for we are well able to overcome it" (Num. 13:30). Ten of the other spies, however, spoke words of fear:

> We be not able to go up against the people; for they are stronger than we....The land, through which we have gone to search it, is a land that eateth up the inhabitants thereof; and all the people that we saw in it are men of a great stature. And there we saw the giants, the sons

of Anak, which come of the giants: and we were in our
own sight as grasshoppers, and so we were in their sight.
—NUMBERS 13:31–33

The fear of the ten spies was revealed by their words—and
the Bible calls their words "an evil report" (v. 32). Caleb was
different. Faith in Caleb's heart came out through his words.

You can either talk yourself out of a blessing or talk yourself into one.

You speak what you believe. Second
Corinthians 4:13 says, "We also believe,
and therefore speak." Faith in the heart
will be revealed through the tongue.
Words of faith release God's power; words
of fear limit and destroy. You choose
your outcome by your confession, so don't get hung by your
tongue. The Israelites received what they said. They said they
couldn't take the land, so they didn't. Caleb, on the other
hand, said they could take the land, and he inherited the
promise. Caleb eventually inherited his mountain because
he believed and he spoke it. You can either talk yourself out
of a blessing or talk yourself into one.

Discipline your mouth to speak only what agrees with
God and builds up. One of the reasons I love the prophetic is
that "he that prophesieth speaketh unto men to edification"
(1 Cor. 14:3). Prophecy is about building up. It's edification.
It's exhortation. It's encouragement. It's comfort.

Speak what God says, even if your feelings don't align yet. I
challenge you: Go one full day without saying anything negative. If you're used to speaking negatively, discipline yourself
to go an entire day without speaking anything negative. Don't
criticize anyone. Don't murmur. Don't complain. If you do say
something negative, write it down to increase your awareness.

Another way to keep from being hung by your tongue is to speak the Word of God. Isaiah 55:11 says, "So shall my word be that goeth forth out of my mouth: it shall not return unto me void, but it shall accomplish that which I please, and it shall prosper in the thing whereto I sent it." God's Word does not return void; it accomplishes what it speaks. The Word of God is the highest authority. When you speak it, you release divine power. Replace your words with God's Word. The Word aligns you with heaven's power and authority. The more you speak the Word, the more your faith grows. A good exercise is to write five scriptures that you need to confess over your life and speak them daily.

Watch your words. You will be held accountable. Matthew 12:36–37 says, "Every idle word that men shall speak, they shall give account thereof in the day of judgment. For by thy words thou shalt be justified, and by thy words thou shalt be condemned." It's amazing how much we talk about what people do. Be careful with idle words, for not only your actions and deeds but also your words are important and will be judged. Your words matter eternally. Heaven is listening, and so is your future. Idle words are useless and nonproductive; words like these have consequences. Speak with purpose. Speak with faith. Speak with intention. The tongue is a small member, but it controls the course of your life. Your words are seeds—plant wisely, water faithfully, and speak fruitfully.

EXCELLENT SPEECH

You have to learn the power of speaking correctly. You have to learn the power of confession. You have to learn the power of what the Scripture calls excellent speech: speaking correctly, speaking spiritually, and saying the right thing. Proverbs 25:11 says, "A word fitly spoken is like apples of gold in pictures of silver." You have to know when to speak the right word at the right time. You have to know what to say and what not to say. You have to know when to hold your tongue. There's a time to use your voice and a time to be quiet. As Ecclesiastes 3:7 puts it, there is "a time to keep silence, and a time to speak."

Some people comment on everything. Whenever anything happens, they comment on social media. Listen, you don't have to comment on everything. There's a time to be quiet. There's a time to guard your tongue. There's a time to refrain from speaking. You've got to know when to speak and when not to speak. And when you speak, you have to know what to speak and how to say it.

When comments involve slander, backbiting, gossip, and speaking about other people behind their backs, you must refrain from speaking and avoid joining the crowd that speaks words of death. Remember, if you want to have a good life, enjoy good days, experience good things, and have a fruitful season, then you have to guard your tongue.

There's simply no way around it. It takes discipline. You have to guard your mouth. You have to be careful what you say and how you say it. You cannot allow profanity, ungodly speech, or evil talk to come out of your mouth. Even if others do it, you must not if you want to see good things. Don't sabotage your future by the words that come out of your mouth. Don't sabotage what God wants to do in your life by your tongue. Ask the Lord to help you guard your tongue and your mouth. Withdraw from bad speaking, slander, gossip, backbiting, criticism, ungodly speech, and profanity. These are not examples of excellent speech.

There are some people whose every other word is profane.

They use profanity. They curse. They use ungodly speech. Then they look at their lives and see that their lives are a mess. They have bad relationships, and they have bad things happening—yet they continue to use profanity and curse every day.

I know that if you have that kind of tongue, your life will not go well. You won't experience good things. You let anything come out of your mouth because you believe you can speak however you want simply because you're an adult. You think, "No one can tell me what to say." But in reality, you are unruly and ungovernable—not submitted to authority or to God's authority.

If you don't submit your tongue to God, you are not submitted to God. Let me say that again. If you don't submit your tongue to God, you are not submitted to Him. You can claim that the Lord is the Lord of your life. You can speak about being in the kingdom or say that you're saved all you want. But if your tongue is not submitted to the lordship of Jesus Christ—if you say what *you* want to say, when *you* want to say it, and how *you* want to say it—you are not submitted to God. You are in rebellion, and you won't see good things come your way. God brings good things to those who allow Jesus to be the Lord of their lives—not just in words. When Jesus is Lord of your life, you don't just say it; you work to control your tongue, to speak excellently, to submit your words to the authority of God. It's not just saying it; it's about controlling your tongue.

WORDS OF LIFE

In taming the tongue, it is important to know which words you should speak and to understand what excellent speech is. These words will help keep you from being hung by your tongue.

Gracious words

Jesus' words were filled with grace. Luke 4:22 says, "And all bare him witness, and wondered at the gracious words which proceeded out of his mouth. And they said, Is not this Joseph's son?" Gracious words are beautiful words. Gracious words are kind words. Your mouth can be filled with grace. Grace can pour from your lips (Ps. 45:2). Jesus spoke wonderful things that amazed His listeners. They had never heard such speech. Jesus' speech set Him apart from all others.

"The words of a wise man's mouth are gracious; but the lips of a fool will swallow up himself" (Eccles. 10:12). The word *gracious* in Hebrew implies favor, kindness, and goodwill.[7] Gracious words not only are pleasant to hear but also bring peace, healing, and honor. Gracious speech reflects a wise heart; it is careful, considerate, and beneficial to both the speaker and the listener.

Pleasant words

Pleasant words are kind and gracious words. Proverbs 16:24 says, "Pleasant words are as an honeycomb, sweet to the soul, and health to the bones." Such words bring sweetness to a person's life. Jesus exemplified the power of pleasant words in His teachings and interactions. His speech was often characterized by grace, compassion, and understanding. One translation of Proverbs 16:24 says, "Kind words are like honey—enjoyable and healthful" (TLB). Pleasant words bring health to the bones.

Wise words

A wise person doesn't just have knowledge; they know how and when to use it. "The tongue of the wise useth knowledge aright: but the mouth of fools poureth out foolishness" (Prov. 15:2). Wisdom is transmitted through words. Parents impart wise words to their children. Wise individuals share them with their friends and mentees. Counselors and leaders offer wise words.

Fitly spoken words

Proverbs 25:11 says, "A word fitly spoken is like apples of gold in pictures of silver." "Fitly spoken" refers to words that are timely, appropriate, wise, and well chosen. These words are considered beautiful. "Pictures [or settings] of silver" suggests refinement and elegance.

Seasoned words

Seasoned speech is wise and well balanced, not bland or dull; thoughtful and penetrating, not careless or meaningless; and able to preserve truth, resist corruption, and make truth more acceptable to the hearer. Colossians 4:6 says, "Let your speech be always with grace, seasoned with salt, that ye may know how ye ought to answer every man."

Soft words

Soft words are calm and soothing—like a balm to an open wound or a gentle breeze calming a storm. Proverbs 15:1 says, "A soft answer turneth away wrath: but grievous words stir up anger." "Soft" in the Hebrew context implies gentle and tender.[8]

Faith-filled words

Jesus taught that faith can move mountains if spoken with the mouth (Matt. 17:20). This spirit of faith enables believers to speak boldly even in trials, persecution, or weakness: "We having the same spirit of faith, according as it is written, I believed, and therefore have I spoken; we also believe, and therefore speak" (2 Cor. 4:13).

True and faithful words

Revelation 21:5 says, "And he that sat upon the throne said, Behold, I make all things new. And he said unto me, Write: for these words are true and faithful." The phrase "true and faithful" in Greek is *alēthinoi kai pistoi*, meaning genuine, reliable, trustworthy, and unfailing.[9]

Prophetic words

Prophetic words are divinely inspired utterances spoken by someone under the prompting of the Holy Spirit, and they're words that build up, encourage, and comfort: "But he that prophesieth speaketh unto men to edification, and exhortation, and comfort" (1 Cor. 14:3).

Healing words

Healing words are gentle, truthful, gracious, and timely. They comfort, strengthen, and uplift. Proverbs 12:18 says, "The tongue of the wise is health." In Hebrew the word *health* also implies restoration, wholeness, deliverance, refreshing, and cure.[10]

Life-giving words

John 6:63 says, "It is the spirit that quickeneth; the flesh profiteth nothing: the words that I speak unto you, they are spirit, and they are life." The Greek word for *life* is *zōē*, referring to eternal, abundant, spiritual life—the life of God.[11]

WORDS OF DEATH

In taming the tongue, it is equally important to know the words you should *not* speak. Remove such words from your vocabulary. Negative talk is like poison—it infects you and others.

Corrupt words

Corrupt words are toxic, damaging, and spiritually unhealthy. They include gossip, slander, vulgarity, lying, deceit, critical words, and divisive speech. Ephesians 4:29 says, "Let no corrupt communication proceed out of your mouth, but that which is good to the use of edifying, that it may minister grace unto the hearers." The word *corrupt—sapros* in Greek—means rotten, putrefied, unwholesome, or of poor quality—foul, like spoiled food.[12]

Vain words

Vain words are empty, worthless, misleading, and devoid of spiritual truth or moral weight. "Let no man deceive you with vain words: for because of these things cometh the wrath of God upon the children of disobedience" (Eph. 5:6).

Idle words

As discussed previously, Matthew 12:36 says, "But I say unto you, That every idle word that men shall speak, they shall give account thereof in the day of judgment." The Greek word for *idle—argos—*means lazy, useless, careless, or barren.[13] Idle words lack purpose, value, or truth. Idle words, as with all words, reveal the condition of the heart.

Harsh or grievous words

Harsh words may provide momentary satisfaction but often cause long-term damage. Proverbs 15:1 says, "Grievous words stir up anger." Grievous words—also translated as "harsh," "painful," or "offensive words" (CSB, AMP, CEB)—provoke, insult, or wound.

Deceitful words

Psalm 52:2 warns, "The tongue deviseth mischiefs; like a sharp razor, working deceitfully." This verse is part of David's rebuke of Doeg the Edomite, who used deceptive speech to betray the priests of Nob, resulting in their slaughter (1 Sam. 22). The phrase shows that deceitful speech is premeditated—intentionally crafted for evil, not merely careless.

Flattering words

Flattering lips speak praise that is exaggerated, insincere, or manipulative. "They speak vanity every one with his neighbour: with flattering lips and with a double heart do they speak" (Ps. 12:2). Flattery deceives, often to gain favor or control.

Profanity

One thing I detest is profanity, and God hates it as well. Profanity—profane words coming out of our hearts and mouths—represents an unclean heart. Proverbs 8:13 says, "The fear of the LORD is to hate evil: pride, and arrogancy, and the evil way, and the froward mouth, do I hate." The term *froward* means perverse, and the Hebrew word applies particularly to speech.[14] You can't say, "I have a pure heart," if you're constantly cursing. A foul mouth reveals a foul heart.

Murmurs and complaints

Don't murmur. Don't complain. These are among the worst things you can do. Philippians 2:14 says, "Do all things without murmurings and disputings." Complaining is, in effect, agreeing with the enemy. Murmuring kept Israel out of the Promised Land. God was displeased with their murmuring because it demonstrated their unbelief. The Israelites murmured and complained in the wilderness; as a result, they never inherited the promise. Stop murmuring and complaining.

Wounding words

Proverbs 12:18 says, "There is that speaketh like the piercings of a sword." The Hebrew word for *piercings* conveys the idea of wounding, thrusting, or stabbing—implying not only offense but intentional or careless harm.[15]

Foolish speech

Don't let your words get you into trouble. Fools run their mouths, and their mouths get them in trouble:

> A prating fool shall fall.
>
> —PROVERBS 10:10

> He that uttereth a slander, is a fool.
>
> —PROVERBS 10:18

> A fool's lips enter into contention, and his mouth calleth for strokes. A fool's mouth is his destruction, and his lips are the snare of his soul.
>
> —PROVERBS 18:6–7

> He that answereth a matter before he heareth it, it is folly and shame unto him.
>
> —PROVERBS 18:13

Foolish speech brings harm to both the speaker and the listener. Don't be a fool. Don't let foolish words come from your mouth. Don't get hung by your tongue by speaking foolishly. Declare:

> *I will live a virtuous life.*
>
> *I will not be hung by my tongue.*
>
> *I will be helped by my tongue.*

I will speak excellent words.

I will speak life.

I will speak blessing.

I will speak words of faith.

I will align my mouth with God's Word.

JohnEckhardtBooks.com/chp5

CHAPTER 6

WORDS OF THE WISE

THE SPIRIT OF God is called the Spirit of wisdom—a divine force that surpasses human intellect. Joshua received the Spirit of wisdom to lead the Israelites: "And Joshua the son of Nun was full of the spirit of wisdom; for Moses had laid his hands upon him: and the children of Israel hearkened unto him, and did as the LORD commanded Moses" (Deut. 34:9). A prophecy about Jesus, the Messiah, in the Book of Isaiah says, "And the spirit of the LORD shall rest upon him, the spirit of wisdom and understanding, the spirit of counsel and might, the spirit of knowledge and of the fear of the LORD" (11:2). The Apostle Paul prayed that "the God of our Lord Jesus Christ, the Father of glory, may give unto you the spirit of wisdom and revelation in the knowledge of him" (Eph. 1:17).

As believers, we should operate in the Spirit of wisdom. When we speak, our words should reflect wisdom. Wisdom is vital. Proverbs 4:7 says, "Wisdom is the principal thing; therefore get wisdom: and with all thy getting get understanding." However, not everything that masquerades as wisdom is wisdom.

WORLDLY WISDOM

A lot of information is available in the world today that many people consider to be wisdom. But worldly wisdom and godly wisdom are not the same thing; in fact, there are times when worldly wisdom is the opposite of godly wisdom. The church cannot operate in worldly wisdom. Men and women of faith cannot operate in worldly wisdom. We must operate in godly wisdom. God's wisdom is higher than man's wisdom. The Apostle James, in the same chapter where he wrote about taming the tongue, stated that man's wisdom "descendeth not from above, but is earthly, sensual, devilish. For where envying and strife is, there is confusion and every evil work" (Jas. 3:15–16). The Bible also says this about man's wisdom:

> Therefore I will once again do a marvelous work among this people, even a marvelous work and a wonder; for the wisdom of their wise men shall perish, and the understanding of their prudent men shall be hidden.
> —ISAIAH 29:14, MEV

> Where is the wise? Where is the scribe? Where is the debater of this age? Has God not made the wisdom of this world foolish?
> —1 CORINTHIANS 1:20, MEV

In contrast, "the wisdom that is from above is first pure, then peaceable, gentle, and easy to be intreated, full of mercy and good fruits, without partiality, and without hypocrisy. And the fruit of righteousness is sown in peace of them that make peace" (Jas. 3:17–18). We need to make sure that we have godly wisdom in our hearts and mouths.

FOOLISHNESS VERSUS WISDOM

We talked a little about foolish speaking in the previous chapter, and the Scriptures have a lot to say about foolish speech. The Book of Proverbs makes a clear distinction between the words of the wise and the words of fools. Fools are known by their words, but so are the wise.

Proverbs 29:11 says, "A fool uttereth all his mind: but a wise man keepeth it in till afterwards." A fool utters all his mind. A fool gives full vent to his spirit, but a wise man keeps himself under control. This verse underscores the idea that you cannot—and should not—say everything that comes to your mind. To do so is a hallmark of foolishness and a lack of self-restraint, often leading to negative consequences.

The fool is characterized by a lack of governance over their tongue and emotions. Impulses dictate their speech, and they give no thought to the impact of their words. Wisdom, on the other hand, involves self-mastery—the ability to hold back and carefully consider what is said.

Spewing out every thought can imply a failure to process, filter, or evaluate them. Not every fleeting idea or emotional surge is worth expressing. Constantly verbalizing every thought reveals a lack of prudence and sound judgment. It can expose ignorance, immaturity, and an inability to understand social norms.

Unfiltered words can be hurtful, damaging relationships and creating conflict. Anger, frustration, and impulsive opinions, especially when immediately verbalized, can wound others deeply. Wisdom recognizes the power of words and prioritizes their constructive uses.

Someone who speaks without restraint often loses credibility and influence. Their words carry less weight, as they are perceived as impulsive and lacking substance. Wisdom recognizes the importance of thoughtful communication and effective engagement.

The wise person does not get hung by the tongue, but the fool does.

Proverbs 29:11 doesn't advocate for repression or inauthenticity. Rather, it champions the virtue of self-control and thoughtfulness in speech. A wise person takes time to process thoughts and emotions before expressing them. They consider the audience, the context, and the potential impact of their words. They understand that silence can be as powerful as speech, and that carefully chosen words, spoken at the right time, carry far more weight than a torrent of unfiltered thoughts.

The wise person does not get hung by the tongue, but the fool does.

WORD OF WISDOM

Before we look further at wise words, I want to look briefly at the spiritual gift called the word of wisdom. First Corinthians 12:8–10 says,

> For to one is given by the Spirit the word of wisdom; to another the word of knowledge by the same Spirit; to another faith by the same Spirit; to another the gifts of healing by the same Spirit; to another the working of miracles; to another prophecy; to another discerning of spirits; to another divers kinds of tongues; to another the interpretation of tongues.

This is a list of gifts of the Spirit, and it includes the word of wisdom. While the word of wisdom will always be composed of wise words, not all wise words are the word of wisdom.

The simple gift of prophecy is for edification, exhortation, and comfort, but apostles and prophets can go beyond these purposes and speak direction, correction, and revelation. They can do this because of other gifts—such as the word of wisdom, the word of knowledge, and faith—which operate through their offices.

Faith ignites the revelation gifts of the word of wisdom, the word of knowledge, and discerning of spirits. The revelation gifts allow us to know something supernaturally. The word of wisdom is supernatural revelation concerning the divine purpose, mind, and will of God. The word of wisdom can operate and flow through prophecy. The word of wisdom can come in a dream, in a vision, as a word from the Lord, through a prophetic utterance, or by an inner impression.

When God gives you a word of wisdom, it's a portion of God's supernatural wisdom that comes at a particular time, especially in a time of crisis or emergency or when you need to make an important decision. Wisdom is important, and you don't need God's wisdom in every situation; you may need a word, a fraction of that wisdom, and that manifestation is called the word of wisdom.

The word of wisdom is connected to the miracle realm. God is the source of all our victories and breakthroughs. He is the source of our wisdom and strategies. When you obey the word of wisdom, it brings you into the miracle realm. The word of wisdom can give supernatural direction, divine strategy, divine solutions, creative ideas, or divine plans, and it can bring breakthrough or release a miracle, especially in a time of crisis or need.

The word of wisdom isn't talked about as much as the word of knowledge, but it is miraculous. For instance, the prophet Elijah told a widowed woman who was in debt what to do. He gave her a word of wisdom: "Go, borrow thee vessels abroad of all thy neighbours, even empty vessels; borrow not a few" (2 Kings 4:3). The widow did what Elijah said. She then followed Elijah's directions and began to pour her one pot of oil into all the vessels she had gathered, filling them all up. Elijah then told her to sell the oil to pay her debt (vv. 4–7). Elijah's instructions to the widow were a word of wisdom. It was divine wisdom, a portion of God's wisdom about what to do in a difficult situation.

Jacob received a word of wisdom concerning the flock that he watched over for his father-in-law. God gave him a word of wisdom on how to bring forth the spotted and speckled animals, which made him wealthy. (See Genesis 30.)

Many other examples of the word of wisdom can be found in Scripture. Just remember that while the word of wisdom is composed of wise words, not all wise words are the word of wisdom.

WISE WORDS

You need to speak wise words. But to speak wise words, you must have wisdom in your heart. "The heart of the wise teacheth his mouth, and addeth learning to his lips" (Prov. 16:23). It's that heart-mouth connection. When you're walking in God's wisdom, hearing from heaven and hearing the voice of God; when you're getting your godly wisdom from above, not earthly or fleshly wisdom; when Christ becomes your wisdom, your heart will grow in wisdom. You will increase in wisdom. When you increase in wisdom, you will also increase in favor.

> For whoso findeth me findeth life, and shall obtain favour of the LORD.
>
> —PROVERBS 8:35

Wisdom is speaking in that verse. Wisdom releases favor. We need wisdom, knowledge, and understanding. Good understanding brings favor (Prov. 13:15).

Wisdom is excellent. Wisdom is the highest thing. Wisdom is superior. God is excellent in wisdom, and He desires for us to partake of this excellency of wisdom. He said,

> Have not I written to thee excellent things in counsels and knowledge, that I might make thee know the certainty of the words of truth; that thou mightest answer the words of truth to them that send unto thee?
> —PROVERBS 22:20–21

Wisdom and knowledge are connected to the truth. Since the Word of God is the source of both wisdom and truth, meditation on the Word uncovers and releases God's wisdom into our hearts. The Word of God is a treasure chest of wisdom and knowledge. It contains an abundance of revelation for every believer. Every believer who desires to enjoy liberty and victory must take time to study the Word of God and ask for revelation. If you want wise words to come from your mouth, you need to put wise words into your heart through the Word of God.

Proverbs teaches us that wisdom cultivates an internal filter, a thoughtful pause between thought and speech. Recognizing that not every mental impulse deserves verbal expression is a crucial aspect of maturity and a pathway to more meaningful and constructive communication. It reminds us that the power of our words lies in their careful selection and mindful delivery.

Here is a list of key scriptures that contrast foolish speech and wise words, demonstrating how the Bible consistently not only warns against the destructive, careless, or senseless use of words by fools but also illustrates what wisdom looks and sounds like:

The wise in heart will receive commandments: but a prating [babbling or talking excessively] fool shall fall.
—PROVERBS 10:8

Wise men lay up knowledge: but the mouth of the foolish is near destruction.
—PROVERBS 10:14

A prudent man concealeth knowledge: but the heart of fools proclaimeth foolishness.
—PROVERBS 12:23

The tongue of the wise useth knowledge aright: but the mouth of fools poureth out foolishness.
—PROVERBS 15:2

The heart of him that hath understanding seeketh knowledge: but the mouth of fools feedeth on foolishness.
—PROVERBS 15:14

Excellent speech becometh not a fool: much less do lying lips a prince.
—PROVERBS 17:7

Even a fool, when he holdeth his peace, is counted wise: and he that shutteth his lips is esteemed a man of understanding.
—PROVERBS 17:28

The wise receive instruction and correction. They seek knowledge and understanding, and they know how to use that knowledge correctly. The wise know when to speak and when to be silent. The wise speak the truth. But look what happens when a person lets foolish words come out of their mouth:

- "A fool's words get him into fights; yes, his mouth calls out for a beating" (Prov. 18:6, CJB).

- "The words of a wise man's mouth are gracious; but the lips of a fool will swallow up himself" (Eccles. 10:12).

- "The wise shall inherit glory: but shame shall be the promotion of fools" (Prov. 3:35).

- "A fool uttereth all his mind: but a wise man keepeth it in till afterwards" (Prov. 29:11).

Wise words do not include idle words (Matt. 12:36); filthiness, foolish talking, or jesting (Eph. 5:4); foolish questions, genealogies, contentions, and strivings about the law (Titus 3:9); nor strife and meddling (Prov. 20:3). These kinds of words are "unprofitable and vain" (Titus 3:9).

The tongue, when uncontrolled, is a source of destruction. James 3:5–6 says, "Even so the tongue is a little member, and boasteth great things. Behold, how great a matter a little fire kindleth! And the tongue is a fire." Words can draw you into arguing and quarreling. A fool will argue about anything. A fool has no problem getting into a quarrel. A fool is contentious. It is honorable for a man to resolve a dispute, but any fool can get himself into a quarrel. Wise people avoid unnecessary conflict; fools thrive on it—just look at social media.

Constant bickering is rarely a good idea. While healthy disagreements can be constructive, frequent quarreling can take a toll on your physical and emotional health and damage your relationships. It's usually better to sidestep pointless arguments and focus on finding solutions that encourage cooperation. We are to have nothing to do with foolish, ignorant controversies that breed quarrels (2 Tim. 2:23).

The wise teach and feed others with their words. The flock of God is fed through words. Proverbs 10:21 says, "The lips of the righteous feed many: but fools die for want of wisdom." The wise nourish people with their words. They instruct and guide others with words. They impart wisdom and knowledge through words.

Wise words also have the power to protect. Proverbs 14:3 says, "In the mouth of the foolish is a rod of pride: but the lips of the wise shall preserve them." The words of fools bring destruction. The words of the wise bring preservation. Your words can destroy you or preserve you: "A fool's mouth is his destruction, and his lips are the snare of his soul" (Prov. 18:7).

The word *destruction* is mentioned fifteen times in the Book of Proverbs. The Hebrew word for *destruction* means ruin, dismay, breaking, or terror.[1] Proverbs gives us wisdom on how to avoid destruction, and much of the wisdom is related to the mouth: "He that keepeth his mouth keepeth his life: but he that openeth wide his lips shall have destruction" (Prov. 13:3). You can avoid destruction by controlling your tongue. Careless speaking will ruin your life.

The right words spoken at the right time are valuable, as seen in Proverbs 25:11: "A word fitly spoken is like apples of gold in pictures of silver." Ecclesiastes 3:7 reminds us that there is "a time to keep silence, and a time to speak." Certain words are important at certain times. It takes wisdom to know the timing, but correctly timed wise words bring joy: "A man hath joy by the answer of his mouth: and a word spoken in due season, how good is it!" (Prov. 15:23). The wise are sensitive to timing, knowing their words have greater impact when the time is right.

Wise words are like refreshing water: "The words of a man's mouth are as deep waters, and the wellspring of wisdom as a flowing brook" (Prov. 18:4). The wise speak words of life: "The law of the wise is a fountain of life, to depart from the snares of death" (Prov. 13:14). Your words matter. Your words are powerful, so speak words of the wise.

WISDOM DECLARATIONS

Let the spirit of wisdom rest on me (Isa. 11:2).

Let me find wisdom and obtain the Lord's favor (Prov. 8:35).

Lord, give me wisdom in every area where I lack (Jas. 1:5).

Give me wisdom and knowledge to speak the truth and speak the right words at the right time.

Through Your wisdom I am delivered (Prov. 28:26).

Through godly wisdom I am preserved (Prov. 14:3).

JohnEckhardtBooks.com/chp6

CHAPTER 7

PROPHETIC WORDS

T HE PROPHETIC MINISTRY gave me greater appreciation for the power of words. I have both released
prophetic words into many lives and received prophetic words and blessings into my own.

When I use the terms *prophecy* and *prophetic word*, I
am simply referring to hearing the voice of the Lord and
speaking His word to others. Every believer should expect to
hear the voice of God, because each of us is a new-covenant
believer. The foundation of the new covenant provides the
basis for developing a prophetic life. Every believer should
expect to speak as an oracle of God. The key is to develop this
ability intentionally; it will not happen automatically. Some
believers doubt whether God will speak to them. Others can
hear His word, but they struggle with speaking out on behalf
of God. We all need more faith to flow in prophecy. We all
must believe what the Word of God says and then act on it.

Prophetic words are powerful, but it is important to
remember to remain scriptural in everything we do. The
Word of God provides safety and protection from the
misuse and abuse of prophecy. Words have power for both
godly and ungodly purposes, so we need to ensure that the

prophetic words we speak come from God and carry spirit and life.

THE POWER OF PROPHETIC WORDS

Second Samuel 23 records the last words of David, "the sweet psalmist of Israel" (v. 1). His last words begin, "The Spirit of the LORD spake by me, and his word was in my tongue" (v. 2). David knew the power of the Word of God:

> The words of the LORD are pure words: as silver tried in a furnace of earth, purified seven times.
>
> —PSALM 12:6

> As for God, His way is perfect; the word of the LORD is proven; He is a shield to all who trust in Him.
>
> —PSALM 18:30, NKJV

That's why David hid the Word of God in his heart. That's why the Word flowed from his mouth and from his pen. Put the Word in your mouth. Put the Word on your tongue. Speak the Word in faith. What you speak with your mouth will enter your heart, and what is in your heart in abundance will come out of your mouth. It's the heart-mouth connection.

> But what saith it? The word is nigh thee, even in thy mouth, and in thy heart: that is, the word of faith, which we preach.
>
> —ROMANS 10:8

> Then the LORD put forth his hand, and touched my mouth. And the LORD said unto me, Behold, I have put my words in thy mouth.
>
> —JEREMIAH 1:9

God puts His words in our hearts and in our mouths. Amazing things happen when these words are spoken. Words from God spoken by those with authority have great impact. God authorizes people to speak on His behalf. The words they speak have heaven's backing.

Jeremiah is an example of God's spokesman. The scope of Jeremiah's prophetic authority is astonishing. His words carried the power to shift nations and restructure kingdoms. Jeremiah's words would root out, pull down, destroy, throw down, build, and plant (Jer. 1:10). Words are used to demolish the works of darkness and establish the purposes of God. When God gives prophetic words, He fulfills them after they are spoken.

God commanded Ezekiel to prophesy to the wind:

> Then said he unto me, Prophesy unto the wind, prophesy, son of man, and say to the wind, Thus saith the Lord God; Come from the four winds, O breath, and breathe upon these slain, that they may live.
>
> —Ezekiel 37:9

When Ezekiel spoke, the winds came. The winds brought life to those who were dead:

> So I prophesied as he commanded me, and the breath came into them, and they lived, and stood up upon their feet, an exceeding great army.
>
> —Ezekiel 37:10

The dry bones came alive, but it did not happen until someone spoke. Words bring life. Words can release breath. This reveals the power of words again.

Ezekiel, a human prophet, was instructed to speak. His

voice became the conduit through which God's life-giving power was released. This highlights the significance of human obedience and participation in God's work. Our words, when aligned with God's will and spoken in faith, can carry divine power.

First Kings 17:1 tells us that "Elijah the Tishbite, who was of the inhabitants of Gilead, said unto Ahab, As the LORD God of Israel liveth, before whom I stand, there shall not be dew nor rain these years, but according to my word." Elijah's words closed the heavens for three years. When fueled by God's Spirit, the spoken word is not merely descriptive but creative and authoritative. Elijah didn't request drought; he announced it.

Words have the power to open and close. Words spoken on earth can affect what happens in heaven. God partners with human voices to execute His purposes. When a believer speaks in alignment with God's Word and will, these words become keys that unlock provision, protection, healing, judgment, or rain.

The prophetic word edifies, exhorts, and comforts (1 Cor. 14:3). These words strengthen and encourage the church. They bring us great comfort in trials. Prophecy serves to exhort; in the Greek *paraklēsis* means to encourage, comfort, and urge toward a particular course of action.[1] Prophetic words can stir hearts, motivate believers, and provide guidance.

We should desire to prophesy and speak as oracles of God (1 Pet. 4:11). We can speak messages from heaven. Prophecy is inspired utterance, and we are to abound in utterance (1 Cor. 1:5).

Second Peter 1:21 says, "For the prophecy came not in old time by the will of man: but holy men of God spake as they were moved by the Holy Ghost." We can speak words, as we are moved by the Holy Ghost. We speak words, as we are filled with the Spirit (Acts 4:8). We speak words, as we are led by the Spirit. We speak words, as we are stirred by the Spirit. These prophetic words are powerful and transforming. These words change lives.

> And be not drunk with wine, wherein is excess; but be filled with the Spirit; speaking to yourselves in psalms and hymns and spiritual songs, singing and making melody in your heart to the Lord; giving thanks always for all things unto God and the Father in the name of our Lord Jesus Christ.
> —EPHESIANS 5:18–20

Being Spirit-filled causes us to speak. The Holy Spirit gives us words to release through our mouths—powerful words that encourage, instruct, and build up. Singing and giving thanks are also expressions of this Spirit-filled speech. Words are connected to the infilling of the Holy Spirit. In Acts 19:6, believers spoke in tongues and prophesied when they were filled with the Spirit.

THE PROPHETIC PLAN FOR YOUR VOICE

Some time ago I came across a message by Pastor Sarah Morgan of Prayer Academy Global. She preached an amazing sermon regarding the books in heaven God has written about each of us. It was a prophetic word unlike anything I had ever heard preached before.

In the message she said there are books in heaven concerning each of us, and that these books needed to be opened and read. She went on to say that many people will look at you and read a line or a chapter from your book but will never read the whole book. Although we can't expect others to know all about what we are called to do, this shows us that we have a responsibility to find out what's in our book so that we can live according to God's plan for our lives.

To further support her ideas, Pastor Morgan quoted Psalm 40:7–8, where Jesus said, "Behold, I come; in the scroll of the book it is written of me. I delight to do Your will, O my God, and Your law is within my heart" (NKJV). This verse refers to the Word of God and the prophetic books that were written and prophesied long ago concerning Jesus' life and ministry. These verses about the book of Jesus' life indicate that He lived according to that prophetic plan, and He fulfilled it. For instance, in Luke 4, when He opened the book, He said, "The Spirit of the LORD is upon Me, because He has anointed Me to preach the gospel to the poor; He has sent Me to heal the brokenhearted, to proclaim liberty to the captives and recovery of sight to the blind, to set at liberty those who are oppressed; to proclaim the acceptable year of the LORD" (vv. 18–19, NKJV). Then He closed the book.

Several key ideas emerge here: Jesus was in the book; the book was about Him; and His life itself was a book. Pastor Morgan mentioned that each of our lives is a book, but they are closed books that need to be opened, read, and understood. Jesus knew who He was and the will of God for His life because He found Himself in the prophetic books of the Bible. In three and a half years, He fulfilled every prophetic promise in the Scripture connected to His calling and concerning His life. He ultimately died on the cross according to the Scriptures.

As Pastor Morgan continued with her message, she revealed that we don't know what is in our own book because we have never read it. We've never sought God about opening our books or allowed Him to do it so He can show us His plan and purpose for our lives. So many of us are closed books. We've never been opened; we've never been read. According to the Book of Revelation, Jesus is the One who has prevailed to open the book.

Pastor Morgan's message was one of the most amazing sermons I've ever heard. I shared it on my Facebook page. I've been preaching for forty years, so I've heard many great messages, but I'd never heard a message quite like Pastor Morgan's, which states that we are all books, and we discover who we are by learning what's in our books.

So many of us are closed books. We've never been opened; we've never been read.

Knowing what is written on the pages of your book is central to understanding how you are impacting the earth with the calling and gifting on your life. Here are a few ways you can discover them:

Prophetic ministry

Prophets and prophecy have a way of causing us to understand our calling, our purpose, and the plans of God, so I always encourage people to receive sound guidance from a prophetic ministry. It is important for you to discover the will and plan of God. Prophets often bring confirmation. In other words, there may be something on your heart, you may be catching a glimpse of something, or you may be seeing through dreams and visions. These experiences may be God's attempt to show you pages from your book.

The right people

Sometimes your purpose comes into view because you connect to the right people. The right people can help you open your book and discover what's in it, especially if they are prophetic. Such people have insight into the plans and purposes of God for your life.

All of us have the Holy Spirit, so the Spirit of God can also show you things about the assignments and plans He has for you. I don't want to imply that you have to depend on a prophet to discover everything you're meant to do. God can reveal things to you directly. Prophets can also bring revelation, confirmation, and clarity, but they never take the place of God.

For example, Samuel anointed David with oil, signifying he was to be the next king of Israel. (See 1 Samuel 16.) He did the same for King Saul. (See 1 Samuel 9.) Sometimes prophets play an instrumental part in helping us discover the plans and purposes God has for our lives.

INSPIRATION OVER DESPERATION

Years ago I read a book that made the point that, to begin discerning the direction God wants you to go in life, you must have an inspired plan. That lesson is important to remember as you seek to determine what God has written in the book of your life. Many people believe they should operate solely on perspiration, telling themselves the following:

- "If I just work hard enough…"

- "If I perspire profusely, I'll have success."

- "If I just keep working, keep doing, I'm going to be successful."

Have you known anyone like this? Instead of operating from inspiration, they operate from desperation.

Rather than being motivated by desperation, we need to be motivated by inspiration. God doesn't want our lives to be dictated by desperation; He wants us to have a plan, and He wants to inspire that plan. He wants to change us from the inside out.

Many people have been taught to go to school, get a degree, get a job, get paid, get a retirement plan, get married, have children, die at a good old age, and go to heaven. But they never really live inspired.

The word *inspiration* means "God-breathed."[2] When God breathes on you—when He blows on you or inspires you to do something—His inspiration could move you to do something that impacts government, business, education, media, the arts, church, or ministry. He is putting words in your heart to reveal to you His plan and purpose for you.

Many people never act on inspiration. God inspires them to do something, but they shut it down and never follow through. They don't move forward in it. They think that maybe what they are sensing is not God—especially when He inspires them to do something different from what everyone else is doing.

Another thing people fall into is trying to live by someone else's inspiration and calling and trying to find their identity in someone else. Serving and following—being part of their ministries, organizations, or businesses—is different from what I mean here. Sometimes God will inspire you to work alongside an individual. He'll inspire you to submit to a mentor or coach. He'll inspire you to work with an apostle, prophet, evangelist, pastor, or teacher. You can get an impartation from them as you are growing and maturing in the thing God has called you to do. But there are things—separate and different from anyone else—that God will also inspire you to do concerning your life.

INSPIRATION BRINGS UNDERSTANDING

Job 32:8 says, "There is a spirit in man: and the *inspiration* of the Almighty giveth them understanding" (emphasis added). The New King James Version says, "And the *breath* of the Almighty gives him understanding" (emphasis added).

This verse tells us that when God breathes on you, when He inspires you, when His Spirit moves on your spirit, He gives you understanding. You begin to understand the plan of God, the purpose of God, and the calling of God through inspiration. When God inspires you to do something—when He speaks prophetic words or a word of wisdom to you—it is one of the most powerful things that can happen. I can hear Him saying, "Open a business, start a charity, get involved in the governmental realm, get involved in education, do something in ministry, create something, innovate something, build something."

Your calling is your pulpit— the place from which you will preach and bring heaven to earth.

Your calling is your pulpit. It is the place from which you will preach and bring heaven to earth. Can you see it? Your business is your pulpit. Your charity or your position in local or national government is your pulpit. If you don't know just what God is calling you to, let Him breathe on you so you will understand His plan. Ask Him to reveal the pages of your life's book. Ask Him to put His Word in your heart.

Then, when the Spirit of God does breathe on you, don't

quench the Holy Ghost. Let God breathe on you. You are a spirit being, and the inspiration of the Almighty gives you understanding.

COMMIT AND BE ESTABLISHED

Proverbs 16:3 says, "Commit thy works unto the LORD, and thy thoughts shall be established." In other words, commit your works, your plans, and whatever you are doing to the Lord, and your thoughts will be established.

Now, I want you to see the connection here. This verse basically teaches that when you commit what you are doing to the Lord, something shifts in your thought life, your mind. This is key because we are steered in a direction based on our thoughts.

In the classic edition of the Amplified Bible, Proverbs 16:3 reads: "Roll your works upon the Lord [commit and trust them wholly to Him; He will cause your thoughts to become agreeable to His will, and] so shall your plans be established and succeed."

So, when you commit your works to the Lord, He will cause your thoughts to become agreeable to His will. This is how you come to know the will of God. Whatever you're planning—your future, your dreams—when God inspires you and you commit that to Him, you say, "Lord, here are my plans." Scripture says, write the vision and make it plain. (See Habakkuk 2:2.) So write your dream. Use the words God has placed in your heart. Write what you're thinking, because sometimes we're inspired but don't know exactly how it will be done. We don't know all the details, so we need God to intervene in our thoughts and cause them to align with His will. Remember, finding your voice means finding God's plan and purpose for your life.

"What is the will of God? What is God's plan for my life?"

To find answers to these questions, your mind must agree with His plans. God works in you, just as His Word says, "It is God which worketh in you both to will and to do of his good pleasure" (Phil. 2:13). God is the One who works in you both to will and to do of His good pleasure. God causes your thoughts—your mind—to align with His will when you commit your works and your plans to Him.

This also means that anything in your plan that is not agreeable to God's will and purpose will fall away. God will zero your thoughts in on exactly what He wants you to do. Then your plans will be established and succeed, because your plans, decisions, and thoughts align with His.

The Contemporary English Version puts Proverbs 16:3 this way: "Share your plans with the LORD, and you will succeed." Psalm 37:5 adds this: "Commit thy way unto the LORD; trust also in him; and he shall bring it to pass."

START WITH GOD

Now, this all seems so simple—and it is. It's not difficult, but many believers have lost the power of this principle, and many have not fully committed to it. We do things on our own and say, "Well, God, if I need You, I'll call on You." Or, "If I get in trouble and things are not going well, I'll call on You."

No. When you receive a prophetic word, you need to begin with God. Do it at the outset. Submit your plan—whether it's related to ministry, business, education, marriage, or relationships—to the Lord from the start, and your thoughts will be established according to His will.

God will energize and inspire your thoughts. He will breathe on your mind, your thoughts, your plans, and your purposes. He will give you inspiration. That's how you begin to succeed and move in God's will and plan for your life.

Again, the Lord can use prophets to give you inspiration, because prophecy is inspired utterance. Whether you consider yourself a prophet, you will find that God uses you in this way. I have taught for years that every believer ought to be prophetic in the sense that we can hear God and do or say what

Finding your voice means finding God's plan and purpose for your life.

He tells us to do or say. When the Spirit of God moves on us, we begin to prophesy inspiration. We begin to speak by the inspiration of the Holy Ghost into someone's life. We are giving them inspiration. All Scripture was God-breathed, or inspired by God (2 Tim. 3:16). Prophecy is the Word of the Lord. When we prophesy, we are speaking the thoughts and mind of God.

When we prophesy over people, we're imparting God's mind and thoughts for their lives, futures, and destinies. Prophecy is powerful, and it's all rooted in inspiration. It demonstrates the power of inspiration.

DISCERNING WHAT GOD WANTS

Being prophetic means more than delivering a string of words that carry a certain sound and make people jump and shout. Prophets have the ability to know what God likes and doesn't like; they just know it by His Spirit. They have an unction. That's why, if you're prophetic and you're in certain ministries, you might feel nothing during worship. You will see people running and falling out, thinking, "Are you kidding me? There is no glory here. This is flesh."

111

Prophetic people know—and you can know, as you are prophetic as well.

Most often, when you have spent enough time with God and gotten to know Him and His presence, you will more often recognize when something isn't God than when it is. For example, when a false prophet shows up and begins to prophesy, you will sense something isn't right. Again, people may be falling out or shaking, but you will feel that something is not right. You know you are thinking and feeling differently than those around you. You might sense all kinds of devils in the room: Leviathan, Jezebel, witchcraft, lust, and perversion.

As a voice of heaven, you have an unction, a fervor, a fire of holiness, that alerts you when something's not right. You are grieved. You are vexed. You may try to shake it off and just go along with the program for a while, but like your heavenly Father, you can't simply accept or be party to anything. You may even spend time praying about it. That *something* you feel is called discernment.

It's what you develop as you draw closer to God, and it becomes sharper the more you become like Him. The more you become like Him, the more you will come to love what He loves and hate what He hates.

Everything can look right on the outside because believers are good at being religious in church. We know how to have church. We know how to sing. We know how to do it all. Many of us have been doing it for years. Everything looks right and sounds right; everybody is up, smiling.

Where pure worship happens is not a matter of being Baptist, Methodist, Catholic, Church of God, Charismatic, or Pentecostal. It's none of those things. True worship is in spirit and in truth. I've been in Baptist churches where I felt the anointing, and then I went to a Pentecostal church and felt nothing. Worship that pleases God has nothing to do with denomination. It depends on the heart; it depends on the people. I don't go by what's on the door. I'm looking for the anointing of God. I'm looking for the glory of God. I'm not looking for who the bishop is, who the pastor is, or how nice the building looks. Those things make no difference to God, and they make no difference to me.

PRAYER TO RECEIVE THE INSPIRATION OF GOD

Father, I thank You that just as each person's voice is unique, there is a unique calling and unique gifting on my life.

Whether it's in business, service, ministry, government, media, or the arts, You are breathing on me, for I am not limited to the four walls of the church. Break me out of that mindset now in the name of Jesus. Though I commit to being in the house of the Lord—because that is where I receive inspiration—I know that my voice can expand beyond it into the mountains of culture.

I commit my way to You so that my thoughts become Your thoughts and my plans, Your plans. Help me know my unique talents and gifts. Help me discover my authentic voice. Let me discover what is on Your heart and what You are breathing on me to do.

As You cause my thoughts to become agreeable to Your will, so shall my plans be established and succeed.

Lord, I trust You with all my heart. I will not lean on my own understanding. In all my ways, I acknowledge You so that You will direct my paths.

I repent for the times when I have failed to do that. Increase my faith to believe You will do all that You promise. Let Your inspired thoughts come into my mind and make my plans and thoughts agreeable to Your will. In Jesus' name, amen.

JohnEckhardtBooks.com/chp7

CHAPTER 8

THE WRITTEN RECORD

BOOKS ARE WORDS. As a reader and an author, I know the power of words and books. Books have changed my life. I have seen others' lives change through writing. The word *author* comes from the Latin word *auctor*, meaning originator, creator, or one who brings about. It is derived from the Latin verb *augere*, meaning to increase, to grow, or to originate.[1] The author is not merely a writer but a source—a person who brings something into being, who causes thoughts, stories, visions, or truths to exist where there was once nothing.

Books possess a unique ability: They transform minds, hearts, and ultimately, lives. Unlike any other medium, they invite us into different worlds, perspectives, and possibilities, with an intimacy that allows for deep personal transformation.

When we open a book, we enter a sacred conversation across time and space. The thoughts of individuals who lived centuries ago or continents away become our companions. Through their words, we experience lives we could never live, cultures we might never encounter, and ideas we might never conceive on our own.

The transformative power of books operates on multiple levels. They expand our knowledge and understanding, introducing us to new concepts and challenging our existing beliefs. They develop our capacity for empathy as we inhabit the consciousness of characters unlike ourselves. They inspire us to action, sometimes subtly shifting our course and other times completely altering our trajectory.

Many of history's most influential figures have pointed to specific books as catalysts for their life's work. Books have sparked revolutions, launched movements, and birthed innovations. A single volume at the right moment can provide clarity, courage, or comfort exactly when needed.

The enduring magic of literature is its ability to transform not just how we think but who we are.

What makes books particularly potent is their demand for our active participation. Unlike passive media consumption, reading requires us to create mental imagery, pause and reflect, and wrestle with challenging ideas. This engagement ensures that books don't merely entertain us; they change us.

Perhaps most powerfully, books remind us that we are not alone in our experiences. There is profound healing in discovering that others have walked similar paths, faced similar struggles, and found their way forward. Books build bridges of understanding between disparate experiences, showing us our common humanity.

In an age of distraction and information overload, the focused attention that books require becomes even more precious. They offer an oasis of depth in a desert of superficiality, inviting us to slow down and reflect on what matters most.

The right book at the right time can indeed change everything—opening doors we never knew existed and revealing possibilities we couldn't previously imagine. This is the enduring magic of literature: its ability to transform not just how we think but who we are.

RECORDS AND RECORDERS HAVE POWER

Two individuals in the Bible are explicitly referred to as recorders—a title used for a royal official or chronicler in the court of the king. The Hebrew word is *mazkîr*, meaning one who reminds, recalls, keeps record, brings to mind, or keeps in remembrance.[2] Jehoshaphat the son of Ahilud was a recorder. He served under King David and later under King Solomon. Second Samuel 8:16 says, "And Joab the son of Zeruiah was over the host; and Jehoshaphat the son of Ahilud was recorder." (See also 2 Samuel 20:24 and 1 Kings 4:3.)

Joah the son of Asaph was a recorder. He served under King Hezekiah. Second Kings 18:18 says, "And when they had called to the king, there came out to them Eliakim the son of Hilkiah, which was over the household, and Shebna the scribe, and Joah the son of Asaph the recorder." Joah is also mentioned as a recorder in 2 Kings 18:37 and Isaiah 36:3, 22.

Recorders were high-ranking court officials responsible for chronicling events, keeping royal records, and possibly advising the king. The recorder in Scripture served as the guardian of the king's history—one who captured the acts, decrees, and movements of the kingdom. Spiritually this reveals the calling to preserve what God has done.

Recorders are keepers of divine testimony. They steward

the memories of the miraculous, the victories of the saints, and the breakthroughs of intercession. They are spiritual scribes who write what the Lord has done so it will not be forgotten. As Psalm 105:5 says, "Remember his marvellous works that he hath done." When you write your story, when you testify, when you declare what God has said, you are functioning in the anointing of the recorder.

THE RECORDER IS A WATCHMAN OF WORDS

A recorder was not merely a writer but a discerner. They listened closely, interpreted accurately, and documented faithfully. This is a picture of a prophetic scribe—one who captures the Word of the Lord and releases it into the earth. Jeremiah was instructed to write in a book all that God spoke to him. Prophetic recorders are watchmen with pens. They are moved by revelation and charged with stewardship of divine utterance. When you write what the Spirit reveals, you partner with heaven to release destiny into the earth.

Recorders stood alongside kings such as David, Solomon, and Hezekiah. They worked within the structure of royal authority, demonstrating a connection to apostolic order and governmental grace. Today's recorders align with apostolic and prophetic movements to bring clarity, administration, and execution of heaven's blueprints. They capture strategy, define seasons, and release insight for leadership. Their writings are more than reflections; they are maps for movement and war scrolls for the advancing church.

To be a recorder was to be trusted with access to the king. It meant standing in the inner court where decrees were released and decisions were made. This is a picture of intimacy and authority. Prophetic recorders live in the presence.

They write from the secret place. They don't just report history; they carry revelation from the throne. Like the Apostle John on the Isle of Patmos, they hear the voice like a trumpet saying, "Write in a book." They write not from opinion but from vision—not from observation but from encounter.

THE WRITTEN WORD TESTIFIES WHEN VOICES ARE SILENT

Records are words. Records are important because words matter, especially when other voices are silent.

> On that night could not the king sleep, and he commanded to bring the book of records of the chronicles; and they were read before the king. And it was found written, that Mordecai had told of Bigthana and Teresh, two of the king's chamberlains, the keepers of the door, who sought to lay hand on the king Ahasuerus. And the king said, What honour and dignity hath been done to Mordecai for this? Then said the king's servants that ministered unto him, There is nothing done for him....Then took Haman the apparel and the horse, and arrayed Mordecai, and brought him on horseback through the street of the city, and proclaimed before him, Thus shall it be done unto the man whom the king delighteth to honour.
>
> —ESTHER 6:1–3, 11

Mordecai was rewarded and promoted because of a book, a record, a chronicle, a written account that carried weight in the courts of kings. In the night season, when the king could not sleep, he commanded the book of records to be brought before him, and there it was written that Mordecai had uncovered a plot and saved the life of the king. Though time had passed and recognition had been delayed, the reward was still attached to the record. The book spoke when no man did. The written word testified when other voices were silent. The record preserved what might have been forgotten. And in that moment, favor was released, honor was commanded, and promotion came to Mordecai because the book was opened.

Words carry memory. Words carry truth. Words preserve history and proclaim destiny. A record is more than ink; it is testimony. It is proof. It is legal. It is prophetic. When something is recorded, it cannot easily be erased. It becomes a witness in time and eternity. Mordecai's faithfulness was not overlooked, though it was hidden for a season. God had allowed the record to be written because He had already appointed the moment of remembrance. And when the book was opened, Mordecai stepped into his reward.

Words carry memory. Words carry truth. Words preserve history and proclaim destiny.

Your labor in the Lord is not in vain. There is a book. Heaven keeps records. Your tears, your prayers, your faithfulness—they are written. Psalm 56:8 says, "Thou tellest my wanderings: put thou my tears into thy bottle: are they not in thy book?" Similarly, Malachi 3:16 says, "A book of remembrance was written before him for them that feared the Lord, and that thought upon his name." Nothing is wasted. Every act of obedience is recorded. At the appointed time, the King of kings will open the book, and reward will be released. Words matter. Records matter. The God who writes is the God who remembers. Like Mordecai, you may have waited, but the book will speak, and your season of honor will come.

The power of the written word played a crucial role in the rebuilding of the temple in Jerusalem:

> And there was found at Achmetha, in the palace that is in the province of the Medes, a roll, and therein was a record thus written: In the first year of Cyrus the king the same Cyrus the king made a decree concerning the house of God at Jerusalem, Let the house be builded, the place where they offered sacrifices, and let the foundations thereof be strongly laid.
>
> —Ezra 6:2–3

The rebuilding of the house of the Lord was resumed because of a record, a scroll, or a decree that had been written and preserved under the authority of King Cyrus. In Ezra 6, we see that what was halted by opposition, intimidation, and accusation was revived because of a search, because of documentation, because of something written in the archives of the king. The enemy tried to stop the work, and the adversaries of Judah rose with resistance, but there was a record—there was a written word that could not be reversed. The decree of Cyrus had authorized the building, commanded the resources, and endorsed the return. When Darius searched the house of the scrolls, the word was found, and the rebuilding was resumed with even greater authority, protection, and provision. This is the power of what is written. The written decree carried more weight than the threat. The record had power to reverse the delay and reignite the work.

What God commands through kings and prophets, what He records in books and scrolls, cannot be undone by the voice of opposition. Just as the building was revived because of what was written, so God revives your destiny because of what is written. Heaven has a record. God has decreed blessing, release, and restoration over your life. The enemy may accuse, but the written word prevails. The voice of the scrolls overrides the voice of resistance. That's why you must know the decree. That's why you must return to the book. The work resumed because of a record. And your work will resume because of the eternal record written over your life. Let the decree be searched out. Let the scroll be opened. Let the word be declared again. What was halted will be resumed. What was stopped will be restarted. What was frustrated will flourish. Because of the written decree, the house of the Lord shall rise again.

The Apostle Paul understood the power of words. Even near the end of his life, in a cold prison cell, facing the final stretch of his ministry, he said to Timothy in 2 Timothy 4:13, "The cloke that I left at Troas with Carpus, when thou comest, bring with thee, and the books, but especially the parchments." This one verse speaks volumes. It tells us that even in hardship, Paul longed for the written word. He treasured knowledge, revelation, memory, and truth. He knew that what was written carried weight. The cloak would warm his body, but the books would stir his mind, and the parchments would feed his spirit. The parchments were likely sacred writings, perhaps Scripture or even his own notes—his record of what God had revealed. He could not let them be lost. Why? Because words matter. Records matter. Books carry life, instruction, vision, and legacy.

Paul had seen the risen Christ, he had been caught up into the third heaven, and he had cast out demons and raised the dead—yet he still needed the books. He still wanted the scrolls, for God speaks through what is written. "It is written" was Jesus' sword against the enemy, and Paul carried the same understanding. Words live. Words teach. Words endure. Heaven and earth will pass away, but the Word remains forever (Isa. 40:8). Paul's Epistles were words written by inspiration, and today they still shape nations, build churches, and transform lives. What Paul wrote in prison still opens prison doors. What Paul wrote in suffering still brings comfort to the suffering. His words became eternal seed.

Never underestimate the power of a book. Never forget the value of what is written. God gave us a Book. Jesus is called the Word. And your words, your notes, your journals, your parchments may outlive you, just as Paul's did. The written word has a way of carrying revelation into future generations. So write. Read. Keep the parchments close. Words are powerful. What is written will speak, and the Spirit will breathe again on the words of faith, wisdom, and vision entrusted to you.

The Words in a Song

Songs are powerful vehicles for words. When words are set to music, they become easier to remember. The words of songs are found in the Bible. The words were preserved and recorded.

> And he appointed certain of the Levites to minister before the ark of the LORD, and to record, and to thank and praise the LORD God of Israel.
> —1 Chronicles 16:4

Levites were appointed specifically to record words of thanksgiving and praise to the Lord. Songs are important. Songs have tremendous power because they are more than melody—they are message, they are prophecy, they are spirit, and they are life. Words sung from the heart can break chains, shift atmospheres, release healing, stir faith, cast out fear, and bring heaven into the earth.

The Psalms were songs. David's lyrics were weapons of war, songs of deliverance, and instruments of prophecy. When Elisha needed a word from the Lord, he said, "Bring me a minstrel"—and as the minstrel played music, "the hand of the LORD came upon him" (2 Kings 3:15). Songs carry the hand of God. Songs carry the breath of the Spirit. The words of a song—when anointed—are not just poetry but proclamation. They are decrees wrapped in melody. They are truth with wings.

Words are like arrows shot into the spirit. Paul and Silas sang in a prison cell, and their songs became earthquake-generating, door-opening, chain-breaking declarations (Acts 16:25–26). Miriam sang after crossing the Red Sea, and her words became a memorial of God's deliverance (Exod. 15:21). The words of songs can teach, admonish, and instruct, as Colossians 3:16 says, "Let the word of Christ dwell in you richly in all wisdom; teaching and admonishing one another in psalms and hymns and spiritual songs."

Words in song form dive deep. They stick. They echo. They stir memory. They ignite hope. They are like arrows shot into the spirit. This is why heaven sings, why the redeemed sing, why the angels cry "Holy" in unending chorus. Because songs matter. Songs frame the atmosphere of a home, a church, a generation. When those songs carry the Word and those lyrics are bathed in truth, they do not just entertain— they transform. So guard your songs. Write your songs. Sing your songs. Because the words you write and the words you sing have the power to shape the future, release the glory, and carry the sound of heaven into the earth.

THE PURPOSE OF THE SCRIBES

Scribes were recorders and custodians of pivotal words and documents. They preserved Scripture. They wrote prophecies. They wrote history. They wrote for kings. Scribes knew the value of words.

The word *scribe* comes from the Latin word *scriba*, meaning one who writes or secretary. This word is derived from the Latin verb *scribere*, which means to write.[3] From this root, English words such as scripture, inscribe, describe, manuscript, and prescription are derived—all tied to the act of writing or recording.

In ancient times a scribe was more than a writer. The title carried the weight of intelligence, authority, and stewardship. Scribes were responsible for copying sacred texts, documenting royal decrees, managing official records, and preserving legal and religious knowledge. In Hebrew the word often translated as "scribe" is *sōpēr*, which means counter, recorder, or writer, reflecting someone who calculates and transcribes.[4] Scripture features several significant scribes.

Shebna

During King Hezekiah's reign, Shebna the scribe held a high-ranking post in the royal court. He held the office of steward over the royal house (Isa. 22:15)—a role of great authority and trust. Shebna became lifted in pride. He used his position not to glorify God or serve the people but to exalt himself. He carved out a sepulchre for himself on high, seeking to leave a legacy of power and self-glory. However, the Word of the Lord came through Isaiah to rebuke him, declaring that Shebna would be cast out and replaced by a faithful servant, Eliakim. Shebna reminds us that even scribes can go astray if they lose reverence for the words they carry. Authority without humility is dangerous. Words must be stewarded with fear of the Lord—not used to elevate oneself.

Ezra

Ezra the scribe was, by contrast, a man of humble spirit and deep devotion:

> He was a ready scribe in the law of Moses…according to the hand of the LORD his God upon him.…For Ezra had prepared his heart to seek the law of the LORD, and to do it, and to teach in Israel statutes and judgments.
> —EZRA 7:6, 10

Ezra was a reformer. His scribal calling was not only to copy the Law but to live it, teach it, and restore the fear of the Lord in a nation that had strayed. Ezra's words brought revival. His fasting, prayers, and reading of the Book of the Law before the people were acts of spiritual warfare. He was a scribe with clean hands and a pure heart.

Both Shebna and Ezra show us the power of the pen and the weight of responsibility that comes with it. Shebna misused his access to royal records, and his name is remembered with reproach. Ezra honored the Word of God, and his name is remembered with reverence. Words matter. Records matter. Those who handle the Word of God must do so with trembling. The office of the scribe is not about prestige; it is about preserving the voice of God for generations. Let us be like Ezra, faithful scribes who seek, do, and teach the Word so that what we write becomes a bridge to revival—not a monument to pride.

Zadok

Zadok the scribe, though lesser known than Ezra or Shebna, stands as a symbol of sacred duty and faithful recordkeeping in the service of Israel's kings. Mentioned in Nehemiah 13:13, Zadok was appointed by Nehemiah during the restoration after the exile. Entrusted with the treasuries of the house of God, he was charged not merely with administration but with spiritual stewardship. As a scribe, Zadok was responsible for more than numbers—he upheld holy order. He was counted faithful among those selected to oversee the offerings, the tithes, and the storerooms—those things set apart for the Levites and the temple's work.

Scribes like Zadok were not simply clerks; they were guardians of sacred matters. They documented truth, preserved law, and ensured that what belonged to God remained pure. To be a scribe was to serve as a steward of the covenant. Their pens became instruments of order and revival. Zadok's inclusion in the biblical record reveals a man counted trustworthy in a generation rebuilding from ruins.

It was scribes such as Zadok who kept account of sacred offerings, ensured nothing was stolen or wasted, and provided the necessary support for worship. Without such scribes disorder would reign, and the house of God would suffer loss. But faithful scribes maintained divine alignment. Their writings stood as testimonies; their records became safeguards for the community. Though their names are seldom mentioned, they are great in heaven, for they preserved what was holy.

Zadok the scribe reminds us that even in the background—even without a pulpit or title—those who write, record, and guard the house of the Lord are vital to the move of God. In every revival, hidden scribes exist. In every restoration there are faithful recorders. May we rise in the spirit of Zadok: faithful to our assignment, diligent with what is sacred, and committed to the integrity of God's house. For the Lord still honors the scribes who labor in secret, and their words still shape what is built in the earth.

Sheva

Sheva, also known by the variant names Shavsha and Seraiah, served as the royal scribe under King David during one of the most significant eras in Israel's history. Though his role may seem administrative on the surface, this position placed him at the heart of divine destiny. As the royal scribe, Sheva was more than a secretary—he was a custodian of covenant history, a recorder of victories, a guardian of law, and a preserver of worship. His pen followed the moves of a king after God's own heart. He was entrusted with documenting the unfolding of God's kingdom plan on earth through David's reign.

In 2 Samuel 8:17 and 20:25, and 1 Chronicles 18:16, Sheva is listed among David's most trusted officials. While the warriors won battles in the field, Sheva's role was to capture those victories in writing, ensuring that every conquest, every covenant, and every command was preserved for generations. His ink was as vital as the sword. His scrolls became silent witnesses to the rise of a kingdom established by God. It is likely that he documented royal decrees, administrative orders, genealogies, temple arrangements, and even the early frameworks of the psalms of David—sacred songs birthed in the heart of a worshipping king.

Sheva's proximity to David also speaks volumes. He stood near authority; he heard the king's words; he watched the decisions; he understood the weight of leadership and the need for accurate, faithful recording. What he wrote was not simply for the moment—it was for the nation, for the priests, for the prophets, and for the future generations of Israel. His writings would become part of the fabric of Israel's sacred memory, a source of truth and legacy.

To serve as a scribe in David's court was to touch both government and glory, to bridge the natural realm of kingdom affairs and the spiritual atmosphere of divine alignment. Sheva's service reminds us that not all impact is public—some change history by what they record, some shape nations by what they preserve, and some secure legacy by what they write in the quiet.

Today God is still raising up Shevas—scribes who know how to stand near the King, who know how to write the vision, and who preserve truth in a time of deception; men and women whose writing will outlive them, whose faithfulness to record will become fuel for generations. Never underestimate the call of the scribe, for what is written in obedience will shape the kingdom of God on the earth. Sheva was not just a recorder of events; he was a vessel of remembrance, a scribe of glory. His legacy lives on in the scrolls of the Spirit.

Elishama

Elishama the scribe was a man positioned close to power, serving in the court of King Jehoiakim of Judah. He is mentioned in Jeremiah 36:12. After Baruch, the scribe of the prophet Jeremiah, read the words of judgment from the scroll aloud to the people, the matter was brought before the officials. The scroll was then taken to the chamber of Elishama the scribe. His chamber became a place where the Word of the Lord was temporarily stored—a place where prophetic truth was held while kings deliberated and officials consulted.

Elishama's role as a scribe placed him at the intersection of government and prophecy. He was a custodian of written matters, a guardian of scrolls, and one who facilitated communication between the prophetic and the political. Though he did not write the prophecy, he housed it. Though he was not the prophet, he protected the words until they reached their destination. This reveals something powerful—that even those who simply guard the word, those who make room for the scroll, those who hold the revelation in the quiet place, are part of God's divine strategy.

Just like the recorders, the scribes of old were not just writers; they were watchmen. They held truth when others rejected it. Elishama's chamber became a resting place for the Word of the Lord during a time of national rebellion. While Jehoiakim would later burn that scroll in arrogance and pride, the fact remains that for a moment, the Word was safe in the hands of a faithful scribe.

Elishama represents those who understand the value of written truth, those who may never preach in public but guard in private, those who house the word in quiet rooms until God is ready to reveal it. In a generation where the prophetic is often dismissed or mishandled, God is still looking for scribes like Elishama—men and women who will preserve the word, protect the vision, and honor the scrolls of heaven.

Let us be like Elishama—willing to make room for the word, willing to be a hidden part of the unfolding of God's plan. For the scroll must be read, the word must go forth, and the scribes must be faithful. Because words matter. What you preserve today may be the very word that changes a nation tomorrow.

Baruch

Baruch the scribe was more than a mere assistant to the prophet Jeremiah; he was a prophetic scribe, a faithful vessel who wrote the words of the Lord with trembling hands and a loyal heart. Mentioned throughout Jeremiah 36 and other chapters, Baruch is a powerful picture of those who carry the burden of writing in times of national rebellion, spiritual decline, and divine judgment. When Jeremiah received the Word of the Lord in a time when he was shut up and could not go into the house of the Lord, he called Baruch and said, "Take thee a roll of a book, and write therein all the words

What you preserve today may be the very word that changes a nation tomorrow.

that I have spoken unto thee" (Jer. 36:2). So Baruch wrote. He captured every word. He did not alter it. He did not water it down. He recorded the fire and thunder of God's voice as judgment was announced on Judah.

Baruch's writing was not without cost. He risked his life. He faced fear. He was pursued. Yet he remained faithful. He read the scroll in the house of the Lord. He stood before officials. He watched as the king—Jehoiakim—cut the scroll with a penknife and cast it into the fire, piece by piece (Jer. 36:23). But Baruch was not discouraged. The Lord spoke again, and Baruch wrote again. The scroll was rewritten, and even more words were added (Jer. 36:32). This is the perseverance of the prophetic scribe: When the enemy burns the word, the scribe writes again. When men reject the message, the scribe still obeys the mandate.

Baruch reminds us that scribes carry weight in the Spirit. They are not just writers; they are recorders of truth, carriers of divine revelation, and preservers of prophecy. Baruch's pen became a sword. His scroll became a voice. Though he was not the prophet, he bore the prophet's burden. In Jeremiah 45, Baruch was overwhelmed and said, "Woe is me now! For the LORD hath added grief to my sorrow" (v. 3). But the Lord answered him, affirming that though judgment was coming, his life would be preserved (v. 5). God saw Baruch's tears, and He honored Baruch's obedience.

Words matter. Scrolls matter. Scribes matter. Baruch shows us that to write for God is no small thing. It is a sacred call. It is warfare. It is legacy. When you write the Word of the Lord, you join the ranks of Baruch. You carry what heaven says into the earth. You write what must not be forgotten. You speak through ink. You proclaim through parchment. Be encouraged—your writing is not in vain. You may feel hidden, but heaven sees. You may feel pressed, but your scroll is still speaking. The spirit of the scribe is rising, and like Baruch, you will help preserve the Word of the Lord for a generation in crisis.

Shaphan

Shaphan the scribe served during the reign of young King Josiah—one of the most critical and prophetic moments in the history of Judah. He was not a prophet, yet he played a prophetic role. He was not a priest, yet he was instrumental in awakening a generation to the holiness of God. As the secretary, the royal scribe, Shaphan held access to the king, and more importantly access to the scrolls—the ancient writings of the Law that had been long forgotten amid idolatry and spiritual compromise.

During the renovation of the temple, Hilkiah the high priest discovered the Book of the Law, hidden and neglected. It was Shaphan who received this scroll and brought it before the king. Shaphan did not ignore the scroll. He did not treat it lightly. He opened it, read it, and carried the burden of its words. When he read it aloud to Josiah, the power of the written Word shook the palace. The king tore his garments in grief and humility. A deep repentance broke out—not just in Josiah's heart but throughout the land. (See 2 Kings 22.)

Shaphan's faithful reading of the Word became the spark that ignited reformation. His voice carried the weight of ancient covenant. He reminded the nation of what had been written. He became a bridge between the forgotten Word and a generation in desperate need of truth. Without Shaphan the scroll might have remained buried. Without Shaphan's voice, Josiah might not have heard. Without Shaphan's faithfulness, repentance might not have come.

This is the power of a scribe anointed by God. Shaphan didn't just transcribe the Word; he delivered it. He stewarded it with reverence. He read it with conviction. His obedience caused kings to bow, idols to fall, altars to be torn down, and a nation to return to its God.

Shaphan teaches us that words matter, the scroll still speaks, and revival can begin when one person reads the Word with faith and fear. You may not wear a crown, but if you carry the scroll, you carry the key to transformation. Be like Shaphan—open the Book, read it aloud, and let the Word do its work. When the Word is restored, repentance comes. When the Word is honored, revival breaks out. When the Word is read with trembling, heaven responds.

THE POWER OF A LETTER

Philemon is a small book, but it reflects the immense power of words shaped by love, grace, and spiritual confidence.

Paul does not thunder with apostolic command in this letter; instead, he writes with the gentleness of a spiritual father, appealing to the heart rather than issuing demands with authority. He writes to Philemon concerning Onesimus, a runaway slave who has now become a brother in Christ. This letter, though brief, is layered with faith, humility, restoration, and trust.

Paul's words to Philemon are personal, tender, and filled with affection. He calls Philemon a beloved fellow laborer and reminds him of his love and faith toward the Lord and all the saints. Paul does not minimize the offense that had taken place, but he chooses to intercede rather than accuse, to request rather than command. He writes, "Though I might be much bold in Christ to enjoin thee...yet for love's sake I rather beseech thee" (Philem. 1:8–9). This is the power of words seasoned with grace. Paul teaches us that a soft word can open the hardest doors, that loving persuasion can accomplish what force cannot.

Paul's faith in Philemon is evident. He writes not with hesitation but with confidence, saying, "Having confidence in thy obedience I wrote unto thee, knowing that thou wilt also do more than I say" (Philem. 1:21). This is prophetic faith—the language of honor. Paul believed that Philemon would respond with kindness, not just because of the request but because of the love of Christ working in him. Paul's words carried expectation. He believed the Spirit within Philemon would respond to the Spirit in his words.

This short letter is a master class in redemptive communication. It shows that words matter—how they are spoken, how they are written, and how they are received. Philemon is not only a book but a letter that reminds us that relationships can be healed, wrongs can be righted, and people can be restored when the right words are spoken in the right spirit. Paul wrote with wisdom, humility, and love—and his words still speak to us today. They remind us that written words, when led by the Spirit, have the power to transform hearts and shape destinies.

A RECORD FOR THE GENERATIONS

In Isaiah 30:8, the Lord commanded Isaiah: "Now go, write it before them in a table, and note it in a book, that it may be for the time to come for ever and ever." This was not just a message for the moment; it was a record for generations. God told Isaiah to write the Word in a book because the people were rebellious, lying children—children that would not hear the law of the Lord. The written Word would stand as a witness. It would testify even when voices went silent. It would outlast emotion, culture, kings, and time itself.

This was not merely about ink; it was about memory, about judgment, about mercy, and about truth that could not be erased. What is written carries power beyond the moment when words are spoken. Spoken words can be forgotten, but written words live on. They are binding. They are legal. They are prophetic. When Isaiah wrote the Word in a book, he was establishing a witness that would confront rebellion again and again.

A generation may ignore the voice of a prophet, but they cannot escape the power of the written word. It speaks from the shelf. It cries out from the scroll. It reminds, it rebukes, it warns, and it calls to repentance. The Word of God is written because God wanted it to be preserved. Jesus quoted what was written. The apostles stood on what was written. The Spirit still confirms what is written. Isaiah's book still testifies, still speaks to a rebellious people, and still reveals the heart of God and the path of restoration. This is why the enemy hates the written Word. This is why Satan attacks the Bible—why he sows confusion, why he fights literacy and understanding—because written truth cannot be manipulated. It exposes sin; it rebukes error; it reveals righteousness.

So write what God says. Keep a record of the vision. Store up the Word. Your journal, your scroll, your notes—what you write may serve as a testimony to generations. Isaiah obeyed, and his obedience became Scripture. God still calls people to write. Because words matter. Because rebellion must be confronted. Because truth must be remembered. Because what is written will always outlast what is spoken.

God values words so deeply that He commands them to be etched into stone, into scrolls, into books, and into hearts.

Habakkuk was told to "write the vision, and make it plain upon tables, that he may run that readeth it" (Hab. 2:2). With both Isaiah and Habakkuk, the prophet was commanded not only to speak but to write, because what is written carries divine permanence. What is written becomes a memorial, a message preserved beyond the moment, a voice that cannot be silenced. God values words so deeply that He does not leave them to fade into memory. He commands them to be etched into stone, into scrolls, into books, and into hearts.

Writing captures revelation. Writing preserves instruction. Writing testifies against rebellion and stirs faith in the vision. God told Habakkuk to write the vision because vision must be clear, visible, and transferable. Without vision, people perish (Prov. 29:18). The written word is not optional; it is essential. It gives future generations something to run with, something to build with, and something to stand on. The vision written can still ignite revival long after the prophet is gone. The warning recorded can still call a rebellious people to repentance centuries later. Words matter. Books matter. Records matter.

When you write, you obey a prophetic pattern. When you write, you join the company of Isaiah and Habakkuk. You give substance to the invisible. You give structure to the Spirit's whisper. You give future runners the map they need to run their race. So write the vision. Note the warning. Declare the truth. Preserve the prophecy. Because words endure. Words confront. Words instruct. Words ignite. What is written will remain a voice for generations—forever.

The apostles' writings to the churches were not casual letters but divine instruments of instruction, correction, alignment, and encouragement. These letters were not mere opinions or suggestions—these were words birthed by the Spirit, written to establish the foundation of the church, to bring order where there was confusion, to correct what was out of place, and to strengthen weary hearts in the faith. Paul wrote to the Corinthians to set things in order. He wrote to the Galatians to call them back to grace. He wrote to the Ephesians to unveil their identity in Christ. John wrote to assure the believers of eternal life. Peter wrote to stir up remembrance. Every epistle carried weight. Every sentence was pregnant with truth. Every word was written with purpose, for "all Scripture is given by inspiration of God, and is profitable for doctrine, for reproof, for correction, for instruction in righteousness" (2 Tim. 3:16).

Words matter. The apostles understood that what was written would last beyond the moment. They were speaking not only to one generation but to all who would believe. Their writings became the blueprint for holy living, the map for New Covenant order, the defense against heresy, and the sword to cut down false doctrine. Their words are still alive—quick and powerful (Heb. 4:12)—and they still speak. The same letters that corrected Corinth now correct us. The same encouragement written to Philippi now uplifts us. The same rebukes to Galatia now guard us. Why? Because truth is eternal, and words, when written in obedience to God, carry the breath of the Spirit across time.

Be encouraged—your life is being shaped by these words. Be strengthened—your faith is being built by what was written. Just as apostles wrote to bring order to the church, God still sends His Word to bring order to your life. Receive the written Word. Honor the Scriptures. Let them instruct you, correct you, align you, and empower you. For heaven moves through the written Word. What God inspired then still transforms today. Let the Word dwell in you richly (Col. 3:16). Let the letters live. Let the apostles speak again. Because words matter. When they are God-breathed, they carry the authority to change everything.

Words carry power beyond the moment. Psalm 102:18 declares that what is written is not just for today: "This shall be written for the generation to come: and the people which shall be created shall praise the LORD." The psalmist, in a time of affliction and deep travail, was moved to record the dealings of God—not merely for his own comfort but for those who had not yet been born. These are words of legacy, words of witness, and words of praise that will awaken future hearts to the faithfulness of God.

What you write today may be the fire that ignites a generation tomorrow. What you record in your pain may be the strength that upholds someone else in their valley. The psalmist saw by the Spirit that a people would be created—a people not yet walking the earth—and those people would find their voice of praise through the testimony that had been preserved. This is the prophetic power of written words: They outlive circumstances, they outlast suffering, and they rise beyond time.

Every scroll, every journal, every decree, and every scripture has the power to shape those who come after. The Word of God has always been multigenerational. God told Moses to write. He told Isaiah to write. He told Habakkuk to write. He told John to write. Why? Because what is written becomes a foundation. It becomes light in darkness. It becomes direction in confusion. It becomes memory in a time of amnesia.

The written Word is a bridge to the unborn. It allows future generations to stand on the shoulders of faith, to remember what God has done, and to believe for what God will do. The psalmist declares that the response of those generations will be praise. The written word will spark worship. The testimony will birth thanksgiving. The record of deliverance will call forth songs of victory.

So write. Write what God has done. Write what you have seen. Write what you believe. Your words are not in vain. You are not just writing for now; you are writing for the people who shall be created. You are writing for sons and daughters, for seekers and worshippers, and for voices yet to be raised. What is written shall live. What is recorded shall speak. The fruit of your words will be praise in a generation yet to come.

PROPHETIC DECREE FOR
SCRIBES AND RECORDERS

I decree that I am a recorder in the Spirit. I receive divine downloads and revelation from the throne. I write what I hear. I scribe what I see. My hand is anointed to record the will of God. I declare that I preserve prophetic history and proclaim future destiny. My writings align with heaven. I write for kings, generations, and nations. I am a recorder in the King's court, a scribe in His chamber, entrusted with holy assignments, commissioned to document heaven's decrees and release them into the earth.

JohnEckhardtBooks.com/chp8

CHAPTER 9

THE POWER OF CONFESSION

ONFESSING THE WORD of God is one of the most powerful weapons a believer has. It is also one of the ways a believer can exercise authority with words.

The foundational scripture for confession is Proverbs 18:21: "Death and life are in the power of the tongue, and those who love it will eat its fruits" (ESV). This verse is about the power of words. Words are among the most powerful things in the universe. God created the world with words: "Let there be light" (Gen. 1:3). Words are not just sounds; they are spiritual containers carrying breath—carrying life or death, faith or fear, blessing or cursing.

Just as God spoke creation into being, your words shape your world. Hebrews 11:3 says, "Through faith we understand that the worlds were framed by the word of God." Your words can make or break you. The words you speak will either move you forward or hold you back in life.

Many people are trapped by negative confessions: "Nothing ever works for me. Nothing ever works out for me. I'll never be free. I'm always sick. I'll never get a break. Things always go bad for me."

If you are saying these things, you need to change the words coming out of your mouth. Your words have power. Mark 11:23 says, "He shall have whatsoever he saith." You can have what you say. Confession precedes possession. What you consistently say, you will eventually experience. Here's a question: Are your words building a prison or a platform?

PUT THE WORD IN YOUR MOUTH

The most powerful words you can speak are from the Word of God: "For the word of God is quick, and powerful, and sharper than any twoedged sword, piercing even to the dividing asunder of soul and spirit, and of the joints and marrow, and is a discerner of the thoughts and intents of the

Faith cannot operate in a vacuum; it needs fuel.

heart," and "So shall my word be that goeth forth out of my mouth: it shall not return unto me void, but it shall accomplish that which I please, and it shall prosper in the thing whereto I sent it" (Heb. 4:12; Isa. 55:11). Nothing more powerful can come from your mouth than the Word of God. Beyond that it's dangerous to go without the Word of God in your mouth.

The absence of God's Word in your life will rob you of your faith in His ability. Romans 10:17 says, "Faith comes by hearing, and hearing by the word of God" (NKJV). If you're not speaking God's Word, you're likely speaking doubt, fear, and defeat. Faith cannot operate in a vacuum; it needs fuel.

That fuel is the Word. Put yourself in position to receive. Receive from God by speaking His Word into your situation. I love speaking the Word. It is a principle of faith.

Romans 10:8 says, "The word is nigh thee, even in thy mouth, and in thy heart: that is, the word of faith, which we preach." The Word is near to you; it's in your mouth and in your heart. You don't have to go to heaven to bring it down. You don't have to go to hell to bring it up. When the Word gets in your heart, it comes out of your mouth.

God's Word, of course, is His will—His will is His best for you. You align with His will by speaking what He already said. Remember, Isaiah 55:11 says that God's Word will accomplish what He pleases, so speak the Word. Put the Word of God in your mouth.

RELEASE YOUR CREATIVE POWER

Words are how God's creative power is released through you. Genesis 1:26 says, "Let us make man in our image, after our likeness." God released creative power through His words, and man was created in God's image to release creative power with his words.

Now, you're not God, but you're made in the image of God. You were made to speak like God—to release faith-filled words backed by belief. Jesus spoke to a fig tree and said, "Let no fruit grow on thee henceforward for ever" (Matt. 21:19). The next day when Jesus and His disciples came back, the tree was dried up—because Jesus spoke to it. Words are powerful.

When God's Word is conceived in your heart and spoken from your mouth, it becomes a spiritual force. Think of it like this analogy: Your heart is the soil; your words are the seed. Together, they birth God's plan in your life.

Speak what you want to see, not what you see. We walk by faith and not by sight (2 Cor. 5:7). Many people speak what they see or what they feel—they are walking by sight. Instead, speak what you want. Speak hope. Speak faith.

"Faith is the substance of things hoped for" (Heb. 11:1). What are you hoping for? What are you dreaming for? God says, "I told My people they can have what they say, but My people are saying what they have." Either you can have what you say, or you can say what you have. Stop speaking your problem. Start declaring God's promise. Don't call things the way they are. Call things that be not as though they were.

That's a principle of faith. God called things that were not as though they were (Rom. 4:17). You were made in the image of God—so say what you want to see, even if you don't see it yet. That's faith. Here are some practical action steps to shift your confession today:

- Replace "I don't" and "I can't" with "I can do all things through Christ."

- Practice daily confessions, and speak life-giving scriptures over your body, mind, finances, and family.

- Monitor your mouth. Keep a journal or notebook to track when you catch yourself speaking words of death. You may be speaking words of doubt, defeat, and fear more than you realize.

- Renew your mind. Fill your heart with God's Word so your mouth overflows with faith.

Speak life. Speak power. Speak faith. Your tongue is a creative tool. Use it to frame your world with faith. Let God's power be released through your words.

RENEW YOUR MIND;
REPROGRAM YOUR HEART

When you speak the Word of God in faith, it doesn't just inform; it transforms. Death and life are in the power of the tongue. Are you speaking death, or are you speaking life? What are you saying?

Sometimes people subconsciously say things they don't want to happen: "I'm going to die before my time. I'm working myself to death. Everyone in my family died of cancer; I'm probably going to die of cancer too."

They're speaking those statements subconsciously because that's what is deep in their hearts. When that is happening, you need to reprogram your heart. It's like

Your heart is the soil; your words are the seed. Together, they birth God's plan in your life.

reprogramming a computer. You do that by your words. It is the heart-mouth connection that I keep mentioning. It is a vital concept to understanding the power of your words. What is in your heart comes out of your mouth, and what you say will eventually shape your heart. Your heart is your inward man—your subconscious. You need to reprogram it to speak words of life, words of faith, and words of hope. It may take some time to reprogram your heart, but keep saying the Word of God until it's in your heart, and keep speaking the Word of God until it comes out of your mouth subconsciously.

When you make statements such as, "I'm going to die

before my time"—even if it's something you don't want to happen and you are saying it subconsciously—it's dangerous because your body will try to do what your words instruct it to do. Your body and mind will put you in a position to accomplish what comes out of your mouth because they believe that's what you want. They try to direct you in that way because words are powerful and have creative force.

That's why I confess the Word of the Lord daily. I know the Word is in my heart. When facing a situation, the first thing that comes out of my mouth—without thinking—is the Word of God.

My understanding of the power of confession began forty-five years ago with my reading a book by Charles Capps called *The Tongue: A Creative Force*. The power of confession wasn't taught in my church. I didn't know anything about it. But I found this book, read it, and it changed my life. Capps wrote, "God's Word that is conceived in your heart, then formed by the tongue, and spoken out of your own mouth, becomes a spiritual force releasing the ability of God within you."[1]

When I read that book, I began to truly understand the power of renewing my mind and the power of confession—the power of the Word of God coming out of my mouth. Thank God for the power of our words!

Remember, Jesus said,

> Whosoever shall say unto this mountain, Be thou removed, and be thou cast into the sea; and shall not doubt in his heart, but shall believe that those things which he saith shall come to pass; he shall have whatsoever he saith. Therefore I say unto you, What things

soever ye desire, when ye pray, believe that ye receive
them, and ye shall have them.

—Mark 11:23–24

You'll have whatever you say. As previously mentioned, I
know some people preach against that principle. They call
it "blab it and grab it." But Jesus is the One who said it—you
can't argue with the Word. Scripture says you'll have whatever you say. That's the Word of God. I know that sometimes
people can take teachings too far; I understand extremes.
But don't fight against a divine principle that's in the Word
of God by saying, "Well, I don't believe that."

The truth is that if you don't believe it, it probably won't
work for you. Faith must back up your words. Faith works
through the tongue: "We having the same spirit of faith,
according as it is written, I believed, and therefore have I
spoken; we also believe, and therefore speak" (2 Cor. 4:13).
You speak what you believe. So let's do it—let's speak words
of faith and achieve victory.

The principle that a person will receive and have exactly
what they believe and say in life comes straight from
Scripture. It is God's wisdom; it is the Word of God. It is
faith. When you live by this principle, it will change your life.
This is a revelation from God.

The law of faith is believing and speaking. Faith works by
speaking. Faith works by believing in the heart and speaking
with the mouth. It's not just speaking, and it's not just
believing; you must believe that what you say will come to
pass, and you must say what you believe. Your words reveal
your faith—or your doubt.

Words are spiritual containers full of faith or fear, life or
death. Faith-filled words dominate the law of sin and death.

Negative words cancel out your faith. Many people speak defeat, sickness, and lack, and then they live in it. Change your words to change your life.

Don't talk *about* the mountain. Speak *to* the mountain.

In Scripture mountains represent obstacles, barriers, problems, and situations that can appear big—so big that you might think there is no way to overcome them, no way to achieve victory. It doesn't matter whether your mountain is debt, financial problems, sickness, defeat, fear, or anything else. Don't talk about the mountain. Don't talk about how big it is or how bad it is. Don't talk *about* it—speak *to* it. Speak what you desire, according to God's Word.

Faith doesn't go by feelings. Faith goes by the Word of God. Faith goes by what you believe. Faith is the substance of things hoped for (Heb. 11:1). Walk by faith and not by sight (2 Cor. 5:7). Walk by faith and not by feelings. It doesn't mean you won't have feelings. It doesn't mean that your feelings are not real. It just means that your faith is not governed by your feelings.

You are today what you were speaking yesterday, and you'll be tomorrow what you're speaking today.

Begin to confess the promises of God—not the problems of life. Don't confess sickness and give it power. Instead, confess, "I believe I receive healing in my body. I speak life, strength, and wholeness. By His stripes I am healed."

Remember, guarding your mouth is important. Taming your tongue and watching what you say is a discipline you must have. Don't allow idle, careless, or unbelieving speech to come out of your mouth. What you consistently say is what you'll eventually have. The word of faith operates by the Word being in your mouth and in your heart.

Identify areas where your words have limited your life. Repent for speaking words of unbelief or fear. Train yourself to speak God's Word. Speak daily what you want to see manifest. Position yourself to receive God's best by speaking His truth into your life. Be persistent. Don't change your confession based on delays or circumstances. Even if it looks like your circumstances are not changing, walk by faith and not by sight. Don't change your confession—keep speaking it. You are today where your words have brought you. You are today what you were speaking yesterday, and you'll be tomorrow what you're speaking today.

> *God, forgive me for allowing myself to operate in fear, doubt, and unbelief. I repent of it. I renounce it. I turn away from it, and I change my speech. I put Your Word in my mouth. I put Your Word in my heart (Rom. 10:8).*
>
> *Father, I thank You for Your Word in my mouth and in my heart. Lord, Your Word in my mouth and my heart will change my life, change my circumstances. Mountains will be removed because when I speak to mountains, I believe what I say and don't doubt with my heart. I'll have whatever You say, according to Your Word (Mark 11:23).*
>
> *Thank You, Lord, for doing new things for me. I speak new things. The former things have come to pass. New things are declared before they spring forth. You tell me of them (Isa. 43:19; 42:9). I decree new things in my life. I believe for new things. I believe for new breakthroughs, new miracles, new*

anointing, new grace, new favor, new power, new wisdom, new songs, new glory, and new finances. You do great and mighty things for me. You do exceedingly abundantly above all that I ask or think (Eph. 3:20).

Thank You, Lord, for Your Word is in my mouth and in my heart. As I speak Your Word, it manifests. I can have what I say. I am not saying what I see; I am saying what I believe. My faith is the substance of things hoped for, the evidence of things not seen (Heb. 11:1).

JohnEckhardtBooks.com/chp9

CHAPTER 10

DECIDE, DECREE, AND DECLARE

GOD HEARS OUR words: "And the LORD heard the voice of your words" (Deut. 1:34). Psalm 139:4 says, "For there is not a word in my tongue, but, lo, O LORD, thou knowest it altogether." This verse is a powerful reminder of God's all-encompassing knowledge, extending to the words we form in our minds before they are even spoken. It reveals the depth of His intimacy with us and carries a significant ethical implication for the way we communicate. Knowing that God hears and understands every word should inspire us to use speech with greater care, intention, and integrity.

But I have a word for you in this season that will stretch and challenge you: God has given you a unique voice too. God has called you to speak and release specific words into the earth—words that will break things open in people's lives the enemy tried to say were unbreakable. You have a sound that, just like your favorite preacher's, heaven responds to. You have a unique voice that, when used, brings heaven to earth. When you contribute to the world and humanity according to God's will—by finding your purpose and walking in it—you will leave a blessing and legacy on the earth.

It is time for heaven's voice to be heard on the earth. Let this be a new season when the muzzles come off and we feel the Word of the Lord burning within us—like fire shut up in our bones.

Some things will not happen until you open your mouth. Your voice brings heaven to earth. When you open your mouth, heaven speaks. When you prophesy, heaven speaks. When you speak by the Spirit of God, heaven speaks. No matter how much it seems like hell is raging, when you open your mouth, heaven comes.

When you open your mouth, the sick are healed, and demons flee. Miracles and finances are released. When you speak, situations are turned around. Your voice can break every yoke and every barrier.

AUTHORITY IN YOUR MOUTH

A decree is an official order issued by legal authority. Decrees are given by people of authority. Job 22:28 says, "Thou shalt also decree a thing, and it shall be established unto thee: and the light shall shine upon thy ways." All of us have authority, for Jesus Christ "hath made us kings and priests unto God" (Rev. 1:6). Because of Jesus we are all kings and priests. As a king, you have the authority just like kings in the Bible did. As a king through Christ, you have the power to decree things—you have the legal power to issue official orders.

Job 22:28 says, "You will decide on a matter, and it will be done for you, and light will shine on your ways" (EHV). That translation gave me another understanding of decreeing: Decreeing is a decision. When a king issues a decree, he has decided. A king decides something and then decrees it. In Bible times it was often a written decree that was proclaimed throughout the land. Decrees carried weight; they were important decisions.

Sometimes the problem comes when we don't make decisions. You can't decree if you can't decide. You can't decree if your indecision keeps you silent.

You have the power to make decisions in your life. You can choose to change what isn't working. You can decide that you will not keep living as you are. You can begin to decree change. You can decide to speak into your situation. It all begins with a decision.

Sometimes the problem comes when we don't make decisions. You can't decree if you can't decide.

In the beginning—in the Book of Genesis—when darkness covered the face of the deep, God said, "Let there be light" (Gen. 1:3). Before God spoke, He decided. God saw the darkness. He decided to create light and then declared, "Let there be light." Everything begins with a decision. Indecision, or making no decision, will paralyze you in life. "You will decide on a matter, and it will be done for you" (Job 22:28, EHV). "When you promise to do something, you will succeed, and light will shine on your path" (Job 22:28, GW).

What you decide and decree will be established. In other words, your decree opens the way for success, prosperity, and breakthrough to come. The International Children's Bible says, "Anything you decide will be done" (Job 22:28). When you decide, your decision and decree cause it to happen. Because of the power God has given us as kings and priests, our decisions can cause things to change.

The Living Bible says, "Whatever you wish will happen!

And the light of heaven will shine upon the road ahead of you" (Job 22:28). That's an appealing way of putting it into contemporary English. The Message version says, "You'll decide what you want and it will happen; your life will be bathed in light." The Modern English Version says, "You will also declare a matter, and it will be established unto you; and the light will shine upon your ways" (Job 22:28). A decree starts with a decision, but a decree is also a declaration.

Decide. Decree. Declare.

Sometimes the enemy wants to muzzle you. You may get discouraged and stop decreeing, stop speaking. But you must keep using faith-filled words. Faith comes by hearing, but faith is released by speaking.

So keep decreeing. That's why I write so many decrees and confessions, and I put them in all my books. God has given me some unusual decrees because I love searching Scripture and discovering hidden promises we often overlook.

When you read God's promises in Scripture, speak them. Decree those truths in faith. When you put these words in your mouth, I believe you'll see breakthroughs and miracles in your life. Even if life isn't going well, change your confession. Decree in faith. You're a king. You're a priest. You have authority. You have power in the spirit realm. Your words carry power.

When kings made a decree, the entire realm had to obey it. That's the power of a king. The subjects under the king responded to his decree. Remember, in the Book of Esther, Haman had the king issue a decree to destroy all the Jews. Once the king made the decree, he couldn't revoke it. The Jews had to stand up and fight for their lives because a decree had been made for all the people on that day to attack them.

Of course, God delivered them from that demonic decree— just as He wants to deliver you from any demonic decrees spoken against your life. You need to decide, decree, and declare. Break every demonic decree that has been spoken against you in secret or behind your back. No weapon formed against you shall prosper (Isa. 54:17). Every tongue that rises against you in judgment, you condemn. Condemn those tongues—condemn backbiting, curses, and anything uttered in jealousy or hatred. Break it and release the decree of the Lord.

Sometimes God will give you a decree to speak. You can decree over your city, your region, your territory, your family, your children, your finances, or your business. It's a powerful practice that I learned to do many years ago.

When I entered the word of faith movement, I discovered the power of confession, the power of decrees, and the power of speaking in faith. I've practiced this for over thirty-five years and have witnessed miracles and breakthroughs. Sometimes, when we're prophesying over people, prophetic words come forth as decrees that break the assignments of hell and release success.

I encourage you to write your own decrees or use some that I've compiled in my books. *Prayers That Rout Demons* contains many decrees; *Prayers That Activate Blessings* and *Prayers That Release Heaven on Earth* offer even more.

Use decrees to activate the power of your voice. Rise with power and authority—as a king, as a priest of God, as a ruler reigning with Christ. Remember, the kingdom of God is within you (Luke 17:21). The kingdom is in you. Psalm 103:19 says, "His kingdom ruleth over all."

When you speak, you release kingdom dominion and exercise power and authority through your words. Begin today—rise, take your place, and walk in the revelation that you are a king, you have power, you have authority, and you reign with Christ.

Decide. Decree. Declare.

ACTIVATING THE POWER OF THE TONGUE

To be a voice that heaven responds to, you need a certain kind of atmosphere in which to grow, develop, and be stirred—because when you're in such an environment, your gifts, anointing, talents, and abilities come forward. Different factors contribute to this kind of atmosphere, and the local church should be a place where it is cultivated for you to be developed and to grow.

In other words, you should not attend a not-for-prophet church. Though this book is not specifically about the prophetic, anyone who has been called to speak as heaven speaks, or to speak in a way that heaven responds to, must possess a prophetic nature. As previously discussed, to speak into situations and bring heaven instead of hell, healing and peace instead of strife and confusion, to bring the virtue and power of God instead of weakness and defeat, you must be prophetic. To remain built up and stirred in a way that allows you to grow in your ability to be a voice, you must be able to hear from God. This is the core of the prophetic realm. Local churches that accept and promote the prophetic gift and office are the most effective in keeping your voice sharp, accurate, and effective.

If you are in a church that does not cultivate an environment where the glory of God dwells, it may be time to find a new one.

You will not flow in your calling or accomplish your assignments if you are in a church where people fight, shut down, or don't encourage or believe in the prophetic. You will end up dying in that place: You will feel stifled, and eventually you will feel silenced. Having visions and dreams is good, but more than that, to stir your voice and see it impact the nations, you must have a desire for the glory of God.

A voice that brings heaven to earth should want to see God glorified. You should want to see God honored, served, worshipped, and prioritized. Bringing heaven to earth—seeing heaven come into people's lives; seeing heaven come in and change your family and reverse generational curses; seeing heaven come into your church, your city, or your nation—is all about God manifesting His glory, His presence, and the rule of the heavenly realm on earth.

Declaring the glory of God must be your number one priority as you accomplish what God has set you on the earth to do. When you put anything before God, it will disturb the effectiveness of your voice. Expressing the glory of God must be your main concern. If you are in a church that does not cultivate an environment where the glory of God dwells, it may be time to find a new one.

When giving God glory is not our number one priority, we give glory to false gods, just as Israel did. We open the door to idol worship when God is not number one. Our churches and our lives become centers for serving idols and worshipping false gods. We begin breaking covenant and disobeying the voice of God, and the blessing of God is no longer evident. In that environment we compromise our influence in the heavens and on the earth. Many in the church are wondering how we lost the ability to speak into certain areas and see God's power manifest. It is because the glory of God is not the number one priority—we shut it out. If we want to be blessed and see our words carry weight on earth, we must repent and return to a place in our hearts where God is our number one priority. We must give Him glory.

Worship is at the forefront of developing a heart that makes God the priority, because as you glorify God, you become a worshipper. There's no way you can tell me that you glorify God in your life but don't enjoy worship. God's glory is His presence, and He is present in praise and worship (Ps. 22:3). If God is a priority in your life, worship must be important to you. If God is the priority in your life, you must love His presence. If God is a priority in your life, when His presence is in a service, you will not stand there with your hands in your pockets, chewing gum. You will either be bowing down, lifting your hands, dancing, or weeping. True worship should always be the focus in everything you do—your priority should be what exalts God, what brings glory to His name, and what amplifies His nature.

Anytime Israel did not worship God properly, the prophets would come and rebuke them. It was always the will of God for worship not to be relegated to Jerusalem and Israel; it was always meant to go throughout the world so people from every color, tribe, tongue, and language would worship God, because our God is great. There is no one like Him in heaven or on earth. He is awesome. He is magnificent. He is the greatest. He is beautiful. He is majestic. He is powerful. He is the only true and living God. When you receive a revelation of the God for whom you've been called to speak, you'll become a worshipper.

We have the power to create with our words, just as our Father God does. He spoke, and it was so. We speak, and it is so. Our world has been and is shaped by words.

We have the power to speak life or death; we have the power to speak things that were not as though they were. This is why it is so important that we understand not only how we activate heaven with our words but also that we are indeed the heavens, as Paul revealed. So it is time to be activated.

In my book *Prophetic Activation*, I go into depth about the power and practice of activation, especially concerning spiritual gifts specific to prophesying. As you speak, you are first hearing from God what to relay or minister to people—whether at home, in corporate America, or across the nations. What I explain is that to activate something is to start it, trigger it, or set it in motion. Activations are spiritual exercises that use words, actions, phrases, objects, Scripture verses, worship songs, dances, prophetic prayers, and more to trigger the prophetic gifts and help believers in every area of life and ministry to flow freely as they are commissioned to release God's Word on the earth.

Activations set in motion prophetic utterances, songs, and movement that will bring great blessing to the members of local churches, ministries, and communities worldwide.

Activations are designed to break down the barriers that prevent people from operating in prophecy—barriers such as fear, doubt, timidity, and ignorance. They also provide people with opportunities to minister—some for the first time—in a safe and loving environment.

Activations rekindle and fan the flame of ministries that have become stagnant in the prophetic flow. We all need times of rekindling and reigniting. Prophetic activations will ignite believers and churches to prophesy. Motionless churches need to be set in motion. Prophetic activations get us moving again.

That is why I would remind you to stir up (rekindle the embers of, fan the flame of, and keep burning) the [gracious] gift of God, [the inner fire] that is in you by

means of the laying on of my hands [with those of the
elders at your ordination].

—2 TIMOTHY 1:6, AMPC

The value of different activations is that they break your
limitations and give you the ability to operate in different
ways. Don't be limited to your favorite way, but be ready to
move in different ways and administrations. Your expression
of gifts must never become boring and routine; it should
always be exciting and new. God has many surprises for us,
and the prophetic will always release new things.

Activations are not designed to make everyone a prophet—
only God can call and commission a prophet. Activations
are simply designed to stir people to grow in whatever level
they are called to. Among those participating in and leading
activations are prophets, some who have the gift of prophecy,
and others who have the spirit of prophecy due to being filled
with the Holy Ghost. In addition the activations may include
psalmists, minstrels, intercessors, counselors, preachers,
teachers, and dancers. Activations will stir them and cause
them to move more in faith and inspiration. The following
decrees are designed to inspire that kind of activation.

DECREES THAT RELEASE HEAVEN'S VOICE

*Lord, give me strength to bring forth my destiny as
heaven's voice (Isa. 66:9).*

Lord, let me not operate in the wrong spirit (Luke 9:55).

Let me have and walk in an excellent spirit (Dan. 6:3).

Lord, stir up my spirit to do Your will (Hag. 1:14).

I bind Satan, the deceiver, from releasing any deception into my life (Rev. 12:9).

I pray for utterance and boldness to make known the mystery of the gospel (Eph. 6:19).

Lead me and guide me for Your name's sake (Ps. 31:3).

Guide me continually (Isa. 58:11).

Guide me into all truth (John 16:13).

Lead me not into temptation, but deliver me from evil (Matt. 6:13).

Send out Your light and truth, and let them lead me (Ps. 43:3).

Lord, give me wisdom in every area where I lack (Jas. 1:5).

Prayers That Release Revelation

You are a God that reveals secrets. Lord, reveal Your secrets unto me (Dan. 2:28).

Reveal to me the secret and deep things (Dan. 2:22).

Let me understand things kept secret from the foundation of the world (Matt. 13:35).

Let me understand and have revelation of Your will and purpose (Col. 1:9).

Give me the spirit of wisdom and revelation, and let the eyes of my understanding be enlightened (Eph. 1:17–18).

Open my eyes to behold wondrous things out of Your Word (Ps. 119:18).

Let me speak to others by revelation (1 Cor. 14:6).

Let Your Word be revealed unto me (1 Sam. 3:7).

Let Your glory be revealed in my life (Isa. 40:5).

Let Your righteousness be revealed in my life (Isa. 56:1).

Let me receive visions and revelations of the Lord (2 Cor. 12:1).

Let me receive an abundance of revelations (2 Cor. 12:7).

Let me be a good steward of Your revelations (1 Cor. 4:1).

Let me receive and understand Your hidden wisdom (1 Cor. 2:7).

Let me understand the deep things of God (1 Cor. 2:10).

Let my eyes be enlightened with Your Word (Ps. 19:8).

Let me comprehend with all saints what is the breadth and length and depth and height of Your love that I may speak it and minister it to those I am called to (Eph. 3:18).

JohnEckhardtBooks.com/chp10

CHAPTER 11

MIRACLES IN YOUR MOUTH

WHEN GOD CREATED the sun and moon, the act was more than a physical act. In setting the sun to rule by day and the moon to rule by night, God established a prophetic picture of the kingdom. We should be ruling by day. We should be ruling by night. We should have authority. We should walk in the power of the kingdom. So it was not just a celestial phenomenon when He formed the stars; it was a prophetic revelation.

Psalm 19:1 says, "The heavens declare the glory of God." In 1 Corinthians 15:41, Paul also wrote about the glory of the stars and other celestial bodies: "There is one glory of the sun, another glory of the moon, and another glory of the stars; for one star differs from another star in glory" (NKJV). While the sun, moon, and stars declare the glory of God, so do we. We are heavenly people. We sit in heavenly places. The Spirit of God is the heavenly kingdom, and the kingdom of God is within us, so we are the heavens who declare the glory of God. We are carriers of His glory.

Every time you look at the heavens, you should see yourself.

You should see pictures of who you should be. You should see yourself shining bright as the light of the world—full of glory, full of power, and full of splendor. You are not just anybody, though the devil will try to make you think you are. He will beat you down and beat you up. The lies he tells you will cause you to hang your head low if you don't have a revelation about your heavenly identity.

Coming to understand who you are in these new terms may be easier said than done. As you are reading this, you may be saying, "I don't feel like the heavens." We are not talking about feelings. We are talking about faith. Get out of your feelings. This is about faith and what the Word of God says. You must confess this—"I am the heavens"—even though you don't feel like it. You may feel like a total loser, but you'd better start opening your mouth and confessing what God says about you.

Come out of self-pity. You don't have to be a victim. You are not a loser. Begin to say what God says. The devil is a liar. God is about to do something new in your life, and it's going to come by revelation and insight in the Word of God. There are miracles in your mouth. You are so much more impor-tant than you realize. God is trying to show us in Scripture that He created us to live higher than the things of this earth. Don't live below your status. You are the heavens.

THE THINGS ABOVE

You've probably heard people say, "You're so heavenly-minded, you're no earthly good." I don't agree. If you are truly heav-enly-minded, you will do a lot of good on the earth. The problem is that there are not enough heavenly-minded indi-viduals. Instead, many are carnal and earthly. You need to be heavenly-minded, meaning spiritually-minded. You need to manifest the heavens on the earth. What is in heaven? Glory, power, and authority. There is no poverty in heaven. There is no lack in heaven. There is no sickness in heaven. It is possible to have a touch of heaven while you are on earth. Don't settle with hell on earth. Have faith to live like heaven on earth.

The heavens rule over all. Stop looking at yourself as just some earthly person stuck on this planet. You can live above earthly limitations, above the distractions and struggles of this fallen existence. Don't let what is happening on earth bring you down. Don't let earthly people depress you. You can set your mind on higher things and live above it all.

You can praise God. You can have joy. You can speak. You can prophesy. You can pray. You can sing. You can take authority, because you are a part of the heavens. Breakthrough happens in heaven. Healing happens in heaven. In heaven the righteousness, justice, and love of God reign. Heaven is a place where miracle after miracle after miracle take place. In the heavens miracles are normal.

As your mind is set on higher things, you speak as heaven speaks: "As [a man] thinks in his heart, so is he" (Prov. 23:7, NKJV). Think on heavenly things. Think miracles. Think prosperity, deliverance, and shalom.

God is expanding your voice. Your line is going throughout the earth. Everywhere your voice goes, it activates the miraculous. Your voice changes lives and sets free those who are held captive by the enemy.

> Whatsoever things are true, whatsoever things are honest, whatsoever things are just, whatsoever things are pure, whatsoever things are lovely, whatsoever

things are of good report; if there be any virtue, and if
there be any praise, think on these things.

—PHILIPPIANS 4:8

These are the qualities that exist in heaven. These are the characteristics, as voices of heaven, we walk in. Be heavenly-minded and be a great good on the earth.

RELEASING THE MIRACULOUS

I read a book years ago written by John Osteen, the father of Joel Osteen, called *There Is a Miracle in Your Mouth*. I love its title. It's true. There's a miracle in your mouth.

Many miracles can come from your words. Remember, Mark 11:23 says you'll have whatever you say. Your words carry creative power. Miraculous power comes from speaking God's Word aloud. Your words create the atmosphere of your life. Speak life, and life will follow. Speak defeat, and defeat will follow.

Romans 10:8–10 is one of my favorite passages of Scripture. I keep quoting this passage because it is so important to understanding the power of your words:

> But what does it say? "The word is near you, in your mouth and in your heart" (that is, the word of faith which we preach): that if you confess with your mouth the LORD Jesus and believe in your heart that God has raised Him from the dead, you will be saved. For with the heart one believes unto righteousness, and with the mouth confession is made unto salvation.

The Word is near; it's as near as your mouth. The Word of God is right there in your mouth and in your heart. Salvation begins by believing in the heart and confessing with the mouth. That same principle—believing in your heart and confessing with your mouth—applies to healing, deliverance, provision, and purpose. Your words must agree with your beliefs. Your words are seeds. Everything you say is a seed that will produce fruit. Are you sowing seeds of miracles?

Speak what you want to see, not just what you currently feel. Declare God's promises—not the enemy's lies. We create realities with our mouths. Faith must be released through words. Faith is not just believing. It is speaking what you believe. Don't cancel your miracle with negative words. Many people sabotage their miracles by speaking doubt, fear, and unbelief. What you say when you are under pressure determines what you receive when the breakthrough comes. Speak the miracle, not the doubt and defeat.

Psalm 103:20 says, "Bless the LORD, ye his angels, that excel in strength, that do his commandments, hearkening unto the voice of his word." Angels hearken to the sound of God's Word. When you put His Word in your mouth, angels listen. As you declare God's Word, heaven moves on your behalf. When you believe the Word in your heart and speak it from your mouth, you activate the miracles of heaven.

Everything you say is a seed that will produce fruit.

Miracles are in your mouth, so to unlock a miracle, fill your heart with the Word of God. As previously stated, "out of the abundance of the heart the mouth speaketh" (Matt. 12:34). You can't speak life if your heart is full of doubt. You can't speak faith if your heart is full of fear. Fill up on God's Word daily. Speak aloud the promises of God. Make declarations part of your daily routine. Speak healing, favor, victory, restoration, and breakthrough.

A miracle is in your mouth. Speak what God says. Don't be

moved by what you see; be moved by His Word. Your miracle is voice activated. Release it with bold declarations of faith. Confess the Word of God. The following are some examples:

"I will bless the LORD at all times: his praise shall continually be in my mouth" (Ps. 34:1).

The joy of the Lord is my strength (Neh. 8:10).

I confess with my mouth and believe in my heart that Jesus is Lord, and I am saved (Rom. 10:9).

I walk by faith, not by sight (2 Cor. 5:7).

By Jesus' stripes I am healed (Isa. 53:5).

My God will supply all my needs according to His riches in glory in Christ Jesus (Phil. 4:19).

I bring my tithe into the storehouse, and the Lord will open up the windows of heaven and pour out a blessing on me (Mal. 3:10).

I cast all my cares on the Lord, for He cares for me (1 Pet. 5:7).

The peace of God, which surpasses all understanding, will keep my heart and mind through Christ Jesus (Phil. 4:7).

I am more than a conqueror through Jesus, who loves me (Rom. 8:37).

God always causes me to triumph (2 Cor. 2:14).

No weapon formed against me shall prosper (Isa. 54:17).

The Holy Spirit bears witness that I am a child of God (Rom. 8:16).

I am blessed with all spiritual blessings in heavenly places (Eph. 1:3).

I am seated in heavenly places in Christ Jesus (Eph. 2:6).

I am a joint heir with Christ (Rom. 8:17).

The Lord blesses all that I put my hand to (Deut. 28:8).

The favor of God surrounds me like a shield (Ps. 5:12).

Miracles are in your mouth. Speak life, not death. Speak faith, not fear. Speak blessings, not curses. Speak the Word of God, and expect miracles to follow. Release miracles with your mouth.

It is possible to have a touch of heaven while you are on earth. Don't settle with hell on earth.

Your voice releases the goodness of God into the earth. Those under the sound of your voice will be changed, healed, and delivered. God has given you a voice and gifted you in unique ways to spread the gospel—through preaching, teaching, writing books and songs, solving problems, and making the world better. Your gifts are essential to how you will uniquely activate heaven and loose on earth what is loosed in heaven (Matt. 18:18).

I've discovered that God is not limited in what He bestows on us in gifts and talents. The twelve manifestations of the Spirit found in Romans 12 and 1 Corinthians 12 extend beyond just twelve. He can fill us with more than what is described by the fivefold ministry in Ephesians 4. His gifts go far beyond those examples.

Often when you are baptized in the Holy Spirit, God will reveal how He has gifted you in a dream or in a church service. He may speak to you by prophecy with the laying on of hands. He may give gifts to you through an encounter with His glory. Special endowments, gifts, abilities, and talents may also be imparted into your life as you grow and develop.

Every Spirit-filled believer has one special gift, or endowment. Some have more than one. These special endowments lead to miraculous results. As I mentioned earlier, the Amplified Bible even uses the term *special endowments* to describe the gifts given to us, releasing miraculous or supernatural power: "Now about the spiritual gifts [the special endowments given by the Holy Spirit], brothers and sisters, I do not want you to be uninformed" (1 Cor. 12:1).

What can be released through writing, although not one of the spiritual gifts listed in the Bible, is important, because when you have an endowment to write, your books can touch people around the world. A woman was delivered through *Prayers That Rout Demons*; she wasn't a believer, but she came across a copy of the book. I've never ministered to her, but she was delivered through one of my books.

As you explore how God wants to expand and release your voice, you must also stir up the endowments He's imparted to you and move in them because they can bring heaven—deliverance, miracles, and supernatural results—into people's lives. Don't allow anyone to shut down your gift and calling.

SPECIAL ENDOWMENTS FUELED BY SPECIAL FAITH LEAD TO SPECIAL MIRACLES

First Corinthians 12:8–10 lists some of the special gifts of the Spirit:

> To one is given by the Spirit the word of wisdom; to another the word of knowledge by the same Spirit; to another faith by the same Spirit; to another the gifts of healing by the same Spirit; to another the working of miracles; to another prophecy; to another discerning of spirits; to another divers kinds of tongues; to another the interpretation of tongues.

But then verse 28 says, "And God hath set some in the church, first apostles, secondarily prophets, thirdly teachers, after that miracles, then gifts of healings, helps, governments, diversities of tongues." This is where God establishes a distinction in the level of gifting and raises it to special gifts and special endowments. Many of these gifts involve using the power of your words, whether through prayer; speaking words of faith, wisdom, or discernment; or using your words to share your spiritual gift.

Healing

Healing is one of the special endowments. We know that all of us can lay hands on the sick. Every believer can minister healing. Jesus said of all those who believe, "They shall lay hands on the sick, and they shall recover" (Mark 16:18). But in addition there are also gifts of healings—special endowments that give people a greater ability to heal, especially in difficult cases such as cancer, diabetes, or rare diseases.

Such a special endowment is needed today because there

are so many sicknesses and diseases that can be difficult to overcome, especially cancer. But I believe God grants a special endowment to heal cancer. I know people who have been healed of cancer supernaturally through these special endowments.

Miracles

All of us can operate in miracles—because all of us can believe the Word in our hearts and speak it from our mouths. But there is also the special endowment of miracles. Deliverance is a miracle ministry. I believe there are special endowments for deliverance. True miracle-working goes beyond deliverance alone. First Corinthians 12:28 says, "And God has appointed these in the church: first apostles, second prophets, third teachers, after that miracles" (NKJV). Miracles are a ministry. Flowing in this level of ministry indicates you have received a special endowment. In Acts 19:11–12 we see that God worked special miracles by the hands of Paul.

Tongues

Tongues is also a special endowment. Again all of us can speak in tongues due to being baptized in the Holy Spirit. But there is also the gift of diversities of tongues, granting you the ability to speak in tongues on a different level. Such an endowment can operate in intercession, in interpretation of tongues, or in speaking different languages. It is a different level of anointing. When you pray, sing, or minister in tongues, supernatural things can happen. According to 1 Corinthians 14:22, tongues are a sign to unbelievers that can convict them and let them know that God is real.

In the days of the Azusa Street Revival, the endowment of tongues was so strong that when many of the people were baptized in the Holy Spirit, God gave them the supernatural ability to speak a foreign language. They went to countries where that language was spoken and preached and understood the language. We can see the precedent for this set with the apostles after Pentecost.

> And they were all filled with the Holy Ghost, and began to speak with other tongues, as the Spirit gave them utterance. And there were dwelling at Jerusalem Jews, devout men, out of every nation under heaven.
>
> Now when this was noised abroad, the multitude came together, and were confounded, because that every man heard them speak in his own language.
>
> And they were all amazed and marvelled, saying one to another, Behold, are not all these which speak Galilaeans? And how hear we every man in our own tongue, wherein we were born? Parthians, and Medes, and Elamites, and the dwellers in Mesopotamia, and in Judaea, and Cappadocia, in Pontus, and Asia, Phrygia, and Pamphylia, in Egypt, and in the parts of Libya about Cyrene, and strangers of Rome, Jews and proselytes, Cretes and Arabians, we do hear them speak in our tongues the wonderful works of God.
>
> —ACTS 2:4–11

I know of one person to whom God gave the supernatural ability to speak French. She is a Spanish-speaking woman of God who also speaks English, yet she learned French supernaturally. She now speaks and understands it, though she never studied it. Such a manifestation is a special endowment. While most of us must study to learn a language, she simply received the ability.

Faith

I love this next endowment: special faith, or the gift of faith. Romans 12:3 tells us that God gives every person a measure of faith. Special faith, however, enables certain people to believe God for unusual things. It is a level of faith that causes a person to believe God for ridiculous things. I love this gift because it opens the miracle realm and empowers people to believe God for supernatural things.

Knowledge

The special endowment of knowledge is one that God gave to Daniel and the three Hebrew boys. There is both the spirit of knowledge and the word of knowledge—another endowment where you receive knowledge of a particular event, a person, or a situation, past, present, or future. Such an endowment gives you the ability to know things supernaturally. All of us should have knowledge; all of us should study. But there is a spiritual endowment of knowledge where you know things of God on a different level.

Wisdom

One of my favorite endowments is wisdom. Wisdom is the principal thing we all should have. Scripture says in all your getting, get wisdom (Prov. 4:7). Christ is your wisdom (1 Cor. 1:30). If you lack wisdom, ask God for it (Jas. 1:5–6). God gave Solomon a special endowment of wisdom through a dream (1 Kings 3). He received unusual wisdom—greater than any king in history. No king before him or after him possessed the level of wisdom God had given Solomon.

Joshua received an endowment of wisdom when Moses laid his hands on him (Deut. 34:9). Scripture says Joshua was filled with the spirit of wisdom.

Churches can have an endowment of special wisdom. Paul prayed for the Ephesian church to be filled with the spirit of wisdom and revelation (Eph. 1:17). Even as Paul prayed for the church to have wisdom, knowledge, and understanding of the will of God, he also had a revelatory endowment. He had special revelation and insight into the plans and purposes of God above the apostles of his day. In his letters to the first-century church, Paul wrote about these mysteries. He also wrote about understanding, which is an endowment allowing people not only to know the mysteries of God—the deeper things of God—but also to understand them.

These endowments of wisdom, knowledge, understanding, and revelation enable us to know God and the mysteries of the kingdom in deeper ways. I love this endowment because it gives people—preachers, ministers, and believers—a special ability to unlock certain truths in Scripture, to see insights in the Bible beyond the normal interpretation or what's on the surface.

Discernment

Then there's a special endowment of discernment, which is also called discerning of spirits. This endowment gives you the ability to see what other people don't see, to discern the spirit or intent behind an action or behavior—the motive. It enables you to distinguish between what is heavenly and what is earthly, or what is angelic, demonic, or human. It helps you know when God's Spirit is moving and when you're witnessing just a manifestation of the flesh. Discernment is a special endowment all of us should desire. It is also connected to wisdom. All of us should have some measure of discernment, but some of us have a special endowment of discernment, such as those in the office of a prophet or who have a strong prophetic gift.

Mercy

Romans 12 talks about the gift of mercy. It is a special endowment of compassion. It could be compassion for hurting people, homeless people, or people who are in trouble. While I will continue to say that as believers we should all have a measure of the gifts I am discussing, there is a special endowment given to some that, when they operate in their unique and specific gifting, the supernatural—the miraculous—becomes evident.

The gift of mercy and compassion is what drove Jesus to perform miracles among the crowds of people who followed Him. He "was moved with compassion toward them, and he healed their sick" (Matt. 14:13–14). In Matthew 20:30–34, two blind men were sitting by the roadside, "and when they heard that Jesus was going by, they shouted, 'Lord, Son of David, have mercy on us!' The crowd rebuked them and told them to be quiet, but they shouted all the louder, 'Lord, Son of David, have mercy on us!' Jesus stopped and called them. 'What do you want me to do for you?' he asked. 'Lord,' they answered, 'we want our sight.' Jesus had compassion on them and touched their eyes. Immediately they received their sight and followed him" (NIV).

Jesus walked in the miraculous and released all kinds of special miracles that showed the heart of His Father toward mankind. He unlocked the miracles of heaven in people's lives because He has special endowments of mercy, compassion, miracles, faith, healing, and many more. Jesus is our example of what it looks like to fully operate in the supernatural power of God. Through His earthly ministry, He showed what it looks like to release heaven on earth.

When Jesus landed and saw a large crowd, he had compassion on them, because they were like sheep without
a shepherd. So he began teaching them many things.

—MARK 6:34, NIV

Do you feel a strong sense of compassion when you see
the suffering of others—when you see their hurt and broken-
ness? Does it cause you to act on their behalf without giving
any thought about what you will receive in return? Is your
focus on relieving their burdens? You may have the gift of
special mercy, an endowment that leaves supernatural results
when you operate in it.

Giving

The special endowment of giving empowers people with
the ability to give in unusual, supernatural ways. All of us
should give; all of us should sow. But there are givers—people
who can sow large amounts of money—extreme givers whose
giving releases miracles. I've been at conferences where one
person who possessed this gift paid off the whole conference.
I've led conferences where we received offerings that covered
the whole conference budget. All expenses were paid by the
few who were endowed with special giving.

We need to believe God for special endowments like this.
Pastors should not be struggling with budgets and laboring
to raise offerings when these endowments are in the body of
Christ. Women in Jesus' ministry and in the ministry of the
apostles had endowments of giving:

> Certain women, which had been healed of evil spirits
> and infirmities, Mary called Magdalene, out of whom
> went seven devils, and Joanna the wife of Chuza

177

> Herod's steward, and Susanna, and many others, which
> ministered unto him of their substance.
>
> —LUKE 8:2–3

The word *substance* here means possessions, goods, wealth, and property.[1] Lydia (Acts 16) and Phoebe (Rom. 16) in the early church were women of influence and wealth who were patrons and benefactors for Paul's ministry.

Gifts such as this one open opportunities to ministries and keep them from being limited by finances. As the kingdom expands, this gift is increasingly important. You never know who has been given an impartation of extreme giving, but if we are open to this endowment, we will see supernatural results.

Exhortation/encouragement

To exhort and encourage someone out of complacency, defeat, self-doubt, and pity into action, faith, and prosperity is a special endowment. A person with this gift not only moves individuals but also organizations. They are the kind who start movements that instigate ripple effects of change and ultimately can change the world. This gift is connected to a prophetic endowment because, if you remember, the basis of prophetic ministry is "he who prophesies speaks edification and exhortation and comfort to men" (1 Cor. 14:3, NKJV).

Some preachers have this endowment. When they preach, you just get encouraged. When those with this gift teach, you get encouraged. Such individuals have a special endowment to encourage people.

Some people complain that the prophetic ministry of some is too sugary, that they speak too well of circumstances. They would rather hear prophecies of judgment and rebuke. But I like what one leader said in response to this: He said encouragement is lacking in the church.

How can there be too much encouragement? If anything, in some places there is too little encouragement. Is it possible to be overencouraged? Of course, there is a place for prophecies that correct and rebuke. But we need to be encouraged.

This gift is associated with the Apostle Barnabas. He was called the "son of encouragement" (Acts 4:36, NIV). You may have a gift to exhort people, especially the hurting, bruised, afflicted, and discouraged. Exhortation is a special endowment. All of us should exhort and encourage people, but there is a special gift for it that activates supernatural release and breakthrough.

Service/helps

Serving others, also known as the gift of helps, is another endowment found in Romans 12. People with this special endowment assist, help, and serve men and women of God, bringing relief and uplifting the arms of others. Elisha poured water on the hands of Elijah. Aaron and Hur lifted the hands of Moses. We call this supportive ministry. Other expressions of this endowment in the church are ushers, greeters, and administrative staff. This gift extends into the marketplace as well. Administrative, executive, and personal assistants; operations officers; and similar roles can also fit within the expressions of this endowment.

If you are gifted with the gift of service and helps, you bring great blessing to the leadership of your church, group, or organization. You help them fulfill the call and mandate on their lives.

Prophecy

This endowment gives you a greater ability to move in the prophetic. Every believer should be activated in prophecy. We should all "covet to prophesy" (1 Cor. 14:39), and, when we are baptized in the Holy Ghost, we can all move in the prophetic realm. But there is a special endowment of the prophetic. It can operate in singing—a psalmist, for example—or in preaching, teaching, personal prophecy, corporate prophecy, and intercession. Prophecy brings the mind and heart of God into the earth, releasing supernatural results. Great breakthroughs and miracles happen when we operate in these special endowments.

Counsel

Giving people the right counsel, wisdom, and advice is a special gift and endowment. It's known as having a spirit of counsel. From time to time, any one of us can give a good piece of advice. God, Jesus, and the Holy Spirit can give us counsel, and we can share it with others as we've learned principles through our own life experiences. But then there are people who have a special grace, ability, talent, and endowment to counsel. We need them, because "in the multitude of counsellors there is safety" (Prov. 11:14).

Some people need counseling before they make a mistake. Sometimes people get their lives all messed up, and then they go for counseling. But counseling is not only for after you mess up. If you seek wise counsel before you take an action or move into another season of life, it will help you prevent mistakes. It will give you advice before you mess up and give you strategy about your life and your future. Preventive counseling is like having a coach who will walk with you through the journey, helping light the path ahead of you and helping you know what God's will is for your life.

Singing

Singing is another special endowment. In some circles those with this gift are called psalmists. David, Chenaniah, Asaph, Heman, and Jeduthun had this endowment (1 Chron. 15:22; 25:1–9). This not only included prophetic singing but also minstrel or musical endowments. For instance, David was gifted with the harp. He was a skilled player of the harp.

You can be supernaturally endowed in music. Gospel music legend Andraé Crouch supernaturally learned how to play the piano. In 1952, when Andraé was a young boy, his father prayed that God would teach his son to play the piano. Andraé's father was a pastor of a small church that had no musicians. One Sunday, Andraé's father told his son to go sit at the piano, and Andraé just suddenly began to play. He had never taken lessons, and before that moment he had never played the piano. He said, "Somehow I found the tonic note, and my ears just popped open. I started playing, just like that, with both hands! Then the little songs began to come…and they never stopped!"[2]

In the years after that supernatural impartation, Andraé Crouch became one of the premier musical talents in the world. The gift to play the piano was just given to him by God. He went on to write many songs.

Musical, singing, psalmist, and minstrel endowments are needed in the church, because we need people who don't just sing but also open the heavens when they sing. Miracles and breakthroughs occur because they lift their voices or play their instruments using this endowment.

Preaching

I love both teaching and preaching endowments, but I love good preaching. There are some to whom God gives the ability to preach and teach in ways that release the supernatural. Paul had a preaching and teaching endowment. Apollos is another leader from the early church who was mighty in the Scriptures (Acts 18:24, NKJV). He had a strong preaching endowment. Jesus was also anointed by God to preach the gospel (Luke 4:18).

Revelation

There is a revelatory endowment, also known as the spirit of revelation. Paul had this endowment to understand the deeper and mysterious things of God, as was mentioned previously. Such endowments are given to the church, and we need revelatory endowments to move forward in revelation.

Some churches and ministries possess a higher degree of revelation, which can be seen in how they study and divide the Word. It can also come through prayer.

Power and might

There is a spirit of might (chayil)—the spirit by which you can operate in levels of power that produce miracles and healing, as well as powerful preaching, teaching, and services. Remember that power and virtue must operate together to create a righteous and godly balance.

When someone who has the special endowment of might or power ministers, people feel they have just encountered the power of God.

Wealth and finance

Deuteronomy 8:18 says, "For it is He who gives you power to get wealth, that He may establish His covenant which He swore to your fathers, as it is this day" (NKJV). There are endowments for building businesses and wealth. There are endowments for fundraising and philanthropy. I know preachers and ministers who have a special endowment to raise offerings. They have a grace in this area, and it is not just to get money. They know how to stir people to give, so they can receive miracles. They know how to raise the level of giving, so budgets are met.

Scripture says wealth, riches, and joy are gifts of God (Eccles. 5:19–20), so don't feel any shame in walking fully in this endowment, if this is the area in which God has gifted you. The church has a long way to go in understanding blessing, wealth, and financial prosperity.

Prayer

Some people just have a gift of prayer; they have a calling to pray. Epaphras was one who labored fervently in prayer for the Colossian church (Col. 4:12). All of us should pray. We know this—"Men always ought to pray and not lose heart," Jesus told us in Luke 18:1 (NKJV). The church, of course, should pray, but special endowments of prayer are given to prophets, intercessors, dedicated prayer ministries, and those who are given special prayer callings or assignments for certain seasons. This is what distinguishes someone as having a special endowment of prayer.

Evangelism

While all of us should evangelize by sharing the gospel with others to win the lost, there are people with strong evangelistic or revivalistic anointings. Billy Graham, Reinhard Bonnke, and those within my networks, such as Sophia Ruffin and Ryan LeStrange, are great examples of individuals who have strong revivalistic anointings. No matter what they are preaching about, people get convicted and saved. When they preach, the backslider even comes back to the Lord.

Pastoring

Pastors, bishops, overseers, and apostolic overseers, who have the ability to shepherd, watch over, teach, and train people, have shepherding or pastoral endowments.

Pioneering

The pioneering endowment expresses itself in those who plant churches or blaze trails in certain industries and sectors of society. We may see this expressed in the church, as demonstrated by apostolic mothers and fathers who raise up spiritual sons and daughters. They charge and authorize those who are under their leadership. This is a special endowment that some people just carry. When they preach, teach, or even enter a room, their authority in this area is evident.

People were amazed at the authority Christ demonstrated when He preached and cast out devils, and when He spoke to the wind and waves, and they obeyed Him. "What manner of man is this?" they asked each other. (See Matthew 8:27.) Jesus was manifesting this endowment.

This pioneering, apostolic endowment is not just something you can work up or do; it is a level of authority God gives you that is often connected to the office of an apostle or prophet.

Understanding

The ability to understand, comprehend, unravel mysteries, and decode hidden truths—even the secrets of God—is specially endowed by God for His glory. Such abilities help bring solutions to the earth and unlock the mysteries of the kingdom, which are hidden truths, so God's people can prosper and He can be glorified.

Writing

This is one endowment I truly love. Scribes, writers, and authors can operate within the endowment of writing, whereby they write and their books impact people. This is an endowment God has given me. I have an apostolic endowment and a revelatory endowment. These endowments are not gifts I asked for—they are gifts God has given me. I've received them through the baptism in the Holy Spirit, by being involved in inspired environments, and through impartation and prophecy with the laying on of hands, all at certain times in my ministry. I love the writing endowment because it changes lives.

Writing can accomplish what other mediums cannot. God has always appointed and used writers to help people read, connect, and understand Him, His ways, and His will for their lives. The entire Bible was written by people whom God gifted with the writing endowment. Moses had a writing endowment. He wrote the revelations of the Pentateuch. The prophets would have writers and scribes transcribe their revelations into books and letters. Paul had an endowment to write—he wrote the letters to the churches in the New Testament. These writings are in our Bibles. These writings change history, change lives, and bring revelation.

If you have a revelatory endowment, you can write those revelations. You can give insight, understanding, and wisdom through your writing, and when people read your book, they can get activated. As you are endowed with a gift of exhortation, you can exhort and encourage people through your writing. If you have an endowment of wisdom and write the wise sayings and messages God gives you, your wisdom reaches others and helps them live well. If you have a prophetic endowment, you can write prophetically—you can write your visions and dreams.

Dreams and visions

Additionally, there is an endowment for dreams and visions. Daniel had this endowment. Joseph also had this endowment. They both possessed an endowment to interpret dreams.

Do you understand the dream realm? You are specially endowed in this area if you do. You may not understand fully how to operate within this area of gifting. It is special. If you develop it, don't neglect it, and stir it up—if you connect with mentors and leaders who also flow in this area—you will see how it brings supernatural results, miracles, and break-throughs into the lives of those you minister to and serve.

YOUR HEAVENLY GIFTING IS YOUR VOICE

We have covered about twenty-five of the special ways God can uniquely gift His people to bring heaven to earth. You must have the mind of God, which is indeed heavenly-minded, if these gifts are to be a benefit to those you encounter throughout your life on earth. Don't accept it as a criticism when people say believers are of no earthly good because they are heavenly-minded. Scripture says we have the mind of Christ. It also says we are to imitate His life and ministry. Jesus was fully endowed by the Spirit of God in every way; His purpose was to show us the Father and to teach us about the kingdom.

As God begins to stir you in the area in which He has endowed you, begin by knowing you can't limit God. God can give you an unusual endowment that you haven't seen anyone operate in before. He can gift you and someone else with the same endowment, and that endowment could be expressed in different ways because there are diversities of gifts and endowments. There are diversities of tongues and all kinds of diverse workings of miracles. Search the words *divers* and *diversity* as they are used in the Bible. Differences of administrations and differences of operation also exist. You can't put two people in the same box. Depending on the gift mix, one's endowment may operate in a different way from another's.

As God opens your life to His wonders, and as He expands your voice and influence on the earth, continue to study special endowments and how to operate in the special assignments, commissions, mandates, talents, abilities, and gifts that He imparts to you and others. The special miracles, breakthroughs, and supernatural works God can do are exceedingly abundantly above all that we ask or think (Eph. 3:20). There are so many gifts. We all have some of these gifts, and in an apostolic environment these gifts are imparted, activated, stirred up, stretched, and launched. It is amazing how God releases these heavenly gifts to enrich our lives and the lives of those we are assigned to impact.

Pursue the gifts. God does not want you to lack in these endowments. All of them are special, and they result in supernatural breakthroughs and miracles. As we explored these endowments, you may have found yourself saying, "I have that one," yet realized you've neglected it. I challenge you to stir it up. You can be reactivated through prophetic impartation and the laying on of hands. This is why it is so important that you remain connected in a good, prophetic church that has leaders who love to see people prosper.

This is God's heart for you. He wants you to have an abundance of gifts. He doesn't want you to shut Him down because of fear, religion, or tradition. He doesn't want witches and witchcraft to shut His gifts and endowments down in your life. He doesn't want you to die without ever having walked in these special endowments or having witnessed these miracles in your life. He doesn't want you to keep silent when He has placed miracles in your mouth. So pursue your gifts. Seek knowledge and training. Don't be afraid to live above, to live in the heavenly realm. That is your home. You are seated in heavenly places.

Your words matter. Your words are life and spirit. Your words have the power to move heaven. Your words have the power to open and close, to bind and loose. Your words carry the power of deliverance. Your words carry the power to break through. Your words have the power to release God's glory. God has given you a unique voice for such a time as this, and it is time for you to use the power of your words.

PRAYER TO ALIGN YOUR MIND AND GIFTS WITH HEAVEN

Father, I thank You for this word. I thank You for revealing even now all the special gifts and endowments You have given me.

Lord, even as these gifts are wrapped like a beautiful Christmas gift, I pray that You would untie the bow and begin to unwrap the package.

Let it no longer be a package wrapped so that I don't know what the gift is. I pray that by Your Spirit, You will open the package for me, so that I may discover the gifts, talents, abilities, and unique qualities You've put inside me.

As I discover them, let me also walk and move in them. Inspire my thoughts and align my mind with Your mind, so I may know Your plans for me. Let me be heavenly-minded, so I may be of earthly good. Let

all these gifts be revealed to me now in this season
and in the days to come. In Jesus' name, I pray. Amen.

PRAYER TO RELEASE HEAVEN ON EARTH

*Thank You, Lord, for releasing heaven on earth.
Let heaven speak. Let heaven's voice be heard in
every place, every region, every city, every house.
Let the voice of heaven be heard, in the name of
Jesus, on the streets, on the street corners, in the
places of addiction, in the houses of prostitution.
Lord, wherever Your voice needs to go, let it go, in
the name of Jesus. I believe for a release of Your
voice to be heard in every way that brings healing,
blessing, and deliverance. Amen.*

PRAYER TO RELEASE THE
MIRACLES IN YOUR MOUTH

*Father, I thank You that You have placed Your
Word in my mouth and Your Spirit in my heart.
According to Isaiah 59:21, Your covenant is that Your
words will not depart from my mouth, nor from the
mouths of my children and my children's children. I
stand today as one who believes that life and death
are in the power of the tongue (Prov. 18:21).*

*Lord, I ask You to anoint my lips with fire. Purify
my speech so that what I declare aligns with Your
promises. Let my mouth be a fountain of blessing,
not cursing; of faith, not fear; of truth, not lies. I
renounce idle talk, negative confessions, and every*

agreement with doubt. I receive the Spirit of faith that speaks what it believes.

I declare that my mouth is a prophetic instrument. As I decree Your Word, miracles are released. As I proclaim healing, bodies are restored. As I declare provision, resources are unlocked. As I confess deliverance, chains are broken. Let every word I speak under the inspiration of the Holy Spirit carry creative power, just as when You spoke and worlds were formed.

Lord, fill me with boldness to open my mouth wide, knowing You will fill it (Ps. 81:10). Let my decrees establish things in the earth (Job 22:28). Cause my tongue to become like the pen of a ready writer (Ps. 45:1), inscribing destiny, hope, and breakthrough.

Today, I release the miracles in my mouth. I speak life to dead places, light to dark places, and healing to broken places. Let the words of my mouth and the meditation of my heart be acceptable in Your sight, O Lord, my strength and my Redeemer (Ps. 19:14).

JohnEckhardtBooks.com/chp11

A PERSONAL
INVITATION FROM
THE AUTHOR

GOD LOVES YOU deeply. His Word is filled with promises that reveal His desire to bring healing, hope, and abundant life to every area of your being—body, mind, and spirit. More than anything, He wants a personal relationship with you through His Son, Jesus Christ.

If you've never invited Jesus into your life, you can do so right now. It's not about religion; it's about a relationship with the One who knows you completely and loves you unconditionally. If you're ready to take that step, simply pray this prayer with a sincere heart:

> Lord Jesus, I want to know You as my Savior and Lord. I confess and believe that You are the Son of God and that You died for my sins. I believe You rose from the dead and are alive today. Please forgive me for my sins. I invite You into my heart and my life. Make me new. Help me walk with You,

*grow in Your love, and live for You every day. In
Jesus' name, amen.*

If you just prayed that prayer, you've made the most important decision of your life. All of heaven rejoices with you,
and so do I! You are now a child of God, and your journey
with Him has just begun. Please reach out to my publisher at
pray4me@charismamedia.com if you accepted Jesus today or
if this book has encouraged or impacted your life in any way.
We'd love to celebrate with you and send you free materials
to help strengthen your faith. We look forward to hearing
from you!

NOTES

INTRODUCTION

1. Matthias R. Mehl et al., "Are Women Really More Talkative Than Men?," *Science* 317 (2007): 82, https://www.researchgate.net/publication/6223260_Are_Women_Really_More_Talkative_Than_Men.

CHAPTER 1

1. "Lashon Hara (Evil Speech)," My Jewish Learning, accessed July 1, 2025, https://www.myjewishlearning.com/article/gossip-rumors-and-lashon-hara-evil-speech/.
2. Blue Letter Bible, "'āmāl," accessed July 1, 2025, https://www.blueletterbible.org/lexicon/h5999/kjv/wlc/0-1/.
3. Blue Letter Bible, "šāmar," accessed July 1, 2025, https://www.blueletterbible.org/lexicon/h8104/kjv/wlc/0-1/.
4. Blue Letter Bible, "nāḡîḏ," accessed July 1, 2025, https://www.blueletterbible.org/lexicon/h5057/kjv/wlc/0-1/.
5. Blue Letter Bible, "rě'šîṯ," accessed July 1, 2025, https://www.blueletterbible.org/lexicon/h7225/kjv/wlc/0-1/.
6. Blue Letter Bible, "beṭen," accessed July 1, 2025, https://www.blueletterbible.org/lexicon/h990/kjv/wlc/0-1/.
7. Online Etymology Dictionary, "bridle," accessed July 1, 2025, https://www.etymonline.com/search?q=bridle.

CHAPTER 3

1. Blue Letter Bible, "sōtēria," accessed July 1, 2025, https://www.blueletterbible.org/lexicon/g4991/kjv/tr/0-1/.

CHAPTER 4

1. Blue Letter Bible, "ṣāḇā'," accessed July 1, 2025, https://www.blueletterbible.org/lexicon/h6635/kjv/wlc/0-1/.

CHAPTER 5

1. Webster's Dictionary 1828, "virtue," accessed July 1, 2025, http://webstersdictionary1828.com/Dictionary/virtue.
2. Art Katz, "Virtue, Power and Healing," Art Katz Ministries, accessed July 1, 2025, http://artkatzministries.org/articles/virtue-power-and-healing/.
3. Katz, "Virtue."
4. Larry Ellis, "Real Beauty," Larry's Stuff (blog), accessed September 7, 2020, http://www.larryssermonblog.com/414794071.
5. *Merriam-Webster* (thesaurus), "virtue," accessed July 1, 2025, https://www.merriam-webster.com/thesaurus/virtue.
6. Francis P. Martin, *Hung by the Tongue* (F.P.M. Publications, 1976).
7. Blue Letter Bible, "ḥēn," accessed July 1, 2025, https://www.blueletterbible.org/lexicon/h2580/kjv/wlc/0-1/.
8. Blue Letter Bible, "raḵ," accessed July 1, 2025, https://www.blueletterbible.org/lexicon/h7390/kjv/wlc/0-1/.
9. Blue Letter Bible, "alēthinos," accessed July 1, 2025, https://www.blueletterbible.org/lexicon/g228/kjv/tr/0-1/; Blue Letter Bible, "pistos," accessed July 1, 2025, https://www.blueletterbible.org/lexicon/g4103/kjv/tr/0-1/.
10. Blue Letter Bible, "marpē'," accessed July 1, 2025, https://www.blueletterbible.org/lexicon/h4832/kjv/wlc/0-1/.
11. Blue Letter Bible, "zōē," accessed July 1, 2025, https://www.blueletterbible.org/lexicon/g2222/kjv/tr/0-1/.
12. Blue Letter Bible, "sapros," accessed July 1, 2025, https://www.blueletterbible.org/lexicon/g4550/kjv/tr/0-1/.
13. Blue Letter Bible, "argos," accessed July 1, 2025, https://www.blueletterbible.org/lexicon/g692/kjv/tr/0-1/.
14. Blue Letter Bible, "tahpuḵôṯ," accessed July 1, 2025, https://www.blueletterbible.org/lexicon/h8419/kjv/wlc/0-1/.
15. Blue Letter Bible, "maḏqārâ," accessed July 1, 2025, https://www.blueletterbible.org/lexicon/h4094/kjv/wlc/0-1/.

CHAPTER 6

1. Blue Letter Bible, "mᵊḥitâ," accessed July 1, 2025, https://www.blueletterbible.org/lexicon/h4288/kjv/wlc/0-1/.

CHAPTER 7

1. Blue Letter Bible, "paraklēsis," accessed July 1, 2025, https://www.blueletterbible.org/lexicon/g3874/kjv/tr/0-1/.
2. See 2 Timothy 3:16 in the AMP, ESV, and NIV.

CHAPTER 8

1. Online Etymology Dictionary, "author," accessed July 1, 2025, https://www.etymonline.com/search?q=author; "Author etymologies," Anomalogue Blog, August 28, 2011, https://www.anomalogue.com/2011/08/28/author-etymologies/.
2. Blue Letter Bible, "zākar," accessed July 1, 2025, https://www.blueletterbible.org/lexicon/h2142/kjv/wlc/0-1/.
3. Online Etymology Dictionary, "scribe," accessed July 1, 2025, https://www.etymonline.com/search?q=scribe.
4. Blue Letter Bible, "sāp̄ar," accessed July 1, 2025, https://www.blueletterbible.org/lexicon/h5608/kjv/wlc/0-1/.

CHAPTER 9

1. Charles Capps, *The Tongue: A Creative Force* (Harrison House, 1976), 7.

CHAPTER 11

1. Blue Letter Bible, "hyparchonta," accessed July 1, 2025, https://www.blueletterbible.org/lexicon/g5224/kjv/tr/0-1/.
2. Deborah Patterson, "Remembering Andraé Crouch," *Homecoming Magazine*, March/April 2015, https://www.rambomcguire.com/news/2015/6/11/remembering-andrae-crouch.